Making Classroom Inquiry Work

Making Classroom Inquiry Work

Techniques for Effective Action Research

Edited by
Robert P. Pelton

ROWMAN & LITTLEFIELD EDUCATION
A division of

ROWMAN & LITTLEFIELD PUBLISHERS, INC.
Lanham • New York • Toronto • Plymouth, UK

Published by Rowman & Littlefield Education
A division of Rowman & Littlefield Publishers, Inc.
A wholly owned subsidiary of The Rowman & Littlefield Publishing Group, Inc.
4501 Forbes Boulevard, Suite 200, Lanham, Maryland 20706
http://www.rowmaneducation.com

Estover Road, Plymouth PL6 7PY, United Kingdom

British Library Cataloguing in Publication Information Available

Library of Congress Cataloging-in-Publication Data

Making classroom inquiry work : techniques for effective action research / edited by Robert P. Pelton.
    p. cm.
Includes bibliographical references.
  ISBN 978-1-60709-927-7 (cloth : alk. paper) — ISBN 978-1-60709-928-4 (pbk. : alk. paper) — ISBN 978-1-60709-929-1 (electronic)
  1. Action research in education. I. Pelton, Robert P., 1966-
  LB1028.24.M35 2010
  370.72—dc22   2010029866

∞™ The paper used in this publication meets the minimum requirements of American National Standard for Information Sciences—Permanence of Paper for Printed Library Materials, ANSI/NISO Z39.48-1992. Printed in the United States of America

Contents

Preface   vii

Part I: Getting into Your Study

Chapter 1   Action Research: The Essential Strategies   1
               Robert P. Pelton

Chapter 2   Setting the Stage: Understanding the Importance
               of Context in Action Research   13
               David W. Nicholson

Chapter 3   Framing an Action Research Study   43
               Neal Shambaugh, Jaci Webb-Dempsey, Reagan Curtis,
               and Rachel Carpenter Heller

Chapter 4   Qualitative plus Quantitative Data: A Mixed
               Methods Research Design   67
               Diane Davis and Marjorie Leppo

Chapter 5   Action Research Video Studies for Improving
               Classroom Teaching-Learning Performances   83
               Linda A. Catelli

Part II: Planning for Success in Action Research

Chapter 6   Learning Conversations: How Oral Inquiry Supports
             the Five Steps of Action Research   117
             Stefan Biancaniello, Stephanie Cucunato, Sean Biancaniello

Chapter 7   Tools for Collaboration in Action Research   141
             Ellen E. Ballock

Chapter 8   Developing an Action Research Communication Plan   161
             Stephen L. Maltese Jr., Frances Bond, and Barbara Bisset

             Index   181

             About the Contributors   189

             About the Editor   193

~

Preface

Making Classroom Inquiry Work: Techniques for Effective Action Research acknowledges that you, the classroom teacher, are the single most important element in helping every child to succeed in school. This book honors your important role in the education system by giving you the tools to continuously improve the teaching and learning environment for both you and your students. You will find that you can use the action research process and strategies provided in this book to enhance your classroom practices and help you meet your highest teaching goals.

If you are new to action research, I strongly encourage you to read *Action Research for Teacher Candidates: Using Classroom Data to Enhance Instruction* (Pelton 2010). That book was originally written for the teacher-in-training, however its step-by-step approach to action research serves as a primer for anyone new to classroom inquiry. Experienced teachers and school administrators have found that text to be extremely helpful to anyone new to action research.

The book you are about to read takes the action research process to a deeper level. It is intended for the teacher who has an understanding that educating children is not a simple task. This book is for those of you who will not settle for solely focusing on standardized testing to make instructional decisions. It is geared toward those of you who wish to delve deeply into your classroom's needs, your school environment, and your children's learning, by being an action research–oriented teacher. The strategies you will learn will lead to focused, effective, and responsive teaching.

Many educators are now seeing the benefits of using action research as a way to identify classroom needs, integrate the best possible teaching practices, and evaluate teacher effectiveness. Teachers and school administrators are finding that using the action research process is an excellent means of professional development that leads to improved student performance and an overall increase in achievement scores.

The coming pages will address the contextual issues that impact teaching and learning, the negotiations that need to take place while conducting classroom inquiry, and the required planning for a successful study. The authors involved in this book will give you the skills needed to be self directed in your own professional development and make action research a meaningful vehicle for you to bring positive data–documented change to your classroom.

Voice

Throughout this book we will speak directly to the teacher who is in the field and seeks to maximize the potential of his or her own classroom through action research.

Overview

Those of us who have adopted the philosophy and methods of action research have experienced the success of this approach on teaching and learning. The action researchers you will meet within the pages of this book are convinced that you will soon begin to share their enthusiasm for this experiential-based–result-producing process of self-development and pedagogical excellence.

About This Book

The development of this field-based book is a direct result of doing action research. Educators from across practical and pedagogical areas of expertise have come together to reflect upon their own and each other's work in action research. They hold a variety of positions, including college professors, classroom teachers, and some recently graduated interns. Each has explored and integrated best practices and wishes to share the results with you. Every chapter has gone through a series of feedback loops and has evolved into a supportive resource for the classroom teacher. The knowledge we have learned is now yours! Our hope is that it serves you well.

The information in the pages that follow can be used by teachers, teachers-in-training, college supervisors, school supervisors, and specialists in the schools, or by administrators who seek to support teachers or teacher candidates who are learning about and doing their own action research. We believe that anyone who is interested in school-based action research will find this text useful and informative. The driving force behind the development of this text is to provide a user-friendly resource so beneficial that it becomes the most valuable tool in your classroom, serving you as a reference throughout your entire teaching career.

How Is This Text Organized?

Rather than attempting to read this text from cover to cover, begin by skimming the pages. Part I, *Getting Into Your Study*, reviews the fundamental strategies of action research. You will delve deeply into classroom context issues that will help you identify areas for study and plan effective teaching strategies. You will learn how to "frame" your action research within the context of your school and classroom. Additionally, you will learn to use quantitative and qualitative data, along with video studies, to document growth and change in your classroom. This section will help ensure that your action research is well-grounded in the fundamentals of the process.

Part II, *Planning for Success in Action Research*, will help you develop communication skills to make you effective in your classroom inquiry pursuits. You will learn how to use focused conversations and collaboration strategies to maximize your potential while working with others. Finally, you will be guided in developing an action research communication plan, to ensure a successful study.

PART I

GETTING INTO YOUR STUDY

~

CHAPTER ONE

Action Research: The Essential Strategies

Robert P. Pelton

The methods of classroom-based action research are designed to answer the most basic question of teaching and learning: *How well are my students learning what I am teaching?* The central focus of becoming an action research oriented teacher, however, is how you *respond* to that most basic question about teaching and learning. Having feedback and information on your students' learning, including your personal observations and their test scores, is important, but what are you going to do with that data? If your students are meeting the standards, what can you do to enrich their learning? If they are not doing well, what can you do to improve their learning or test results?

Whether you are a new teacher implementing the action research process for the first time, or an experienced teacher sharpening your professional skills, becoming an action research–oriented teacher will make you keenly aware of how to shape your "next steps" for effective instruction.

As you continue to embrace action research as a mindset toward teaching, it should come as no surprise to you that action research–oriented teachers believe that the real solutions for student achievement lie in the expertise of teachers and how they effectively respond to the information, or "data," that is generated by their students in their classrooms each and every day. Action research simply provides an organized, proven, and reliable process for ensuring that you use the data in your classroom to evolve into the high-quality educator that your students need and deserve.

As you know, teaching is not a simple task. You can trust the action research process because is proven to be a highly effective form of professional development. Action research supports the identification and implementation of best practices, assists in the evaluation of teacher effectiveness, and guides teachers to make refinements in their work with children, which in turn has a direct impact on student achievement scores. The chapters thoughout this book will give you strategies to become an exemplary action research–oriented teacher.

Chapter Objectives

By the time you finish reading and thinking about this chapter, you will be able to do the following:

- Discuss the benefits of developing an action research mindset
- Identify the five-step action research process
- Describe how the innate flexibility of action research is a benefit of the approach
- Explain what it is to be a responsive teacher

Key Strategies in Action Research

As you move forward with your classroom inquiry, the following key strategies will help you become an effective action research–oriented teacher:

- Develop the action research mindset
- Utilize a process
- Be flexible to change
- Pay attention to the data
- Collaborate with others
- Be a responsive teacher

Developing the Action Research Mindset (Reflection in Action)

Action research is best seen as a way to approach your work in the classroom and school setting. Think of it as a *mindset* for teaching. It is a powerful mindset because it emphasizes your role as a reflective practitioner who is continually observant, thoughtful, and willing to examine your personal "teacher actions" in the light of best possible practices for your students.

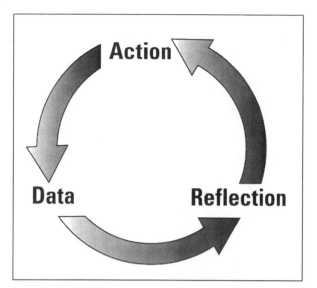

Figure 1.1. Action Research Mindset

Becoming an action research–oriented teacher goes well beyond just doing an action research project.

As a teacher, you have spent a great deal of time reflecting on your actions. Perhaps you have kept a teacher journal, responded to lesson observations, or engaged in other activities as part of your teacher training or as a means to your own professional development.

As an action research–oriented teacher, your reflective skills are going to stretch a little further. Instead of reflecting *on* action, you will be developing the skills of reflection *in* action. In other words, you will train yourself to think about what you are doing *while* you are doing it. The *reflection in action* practitioner considers the impact of his or her actions while they are being implemented—not just after they are implemented or after a marking period concludes. In the course of doing action research, you will grasp the importance of reflecting *while* you are teaching as well as throughout the entire action research process.

Although you will start out following a process for action research, the more you do it, the more it will become part of who you are as a teacher. It will become your mindset for teaching and you will see that you will apply action research intuitively. Ultimately, you will assess your teaching techniques by seamlessly monitoring student learning in a constant cycle of action-data-reflection and then continued action, as shown in figure 1.1. This is what is meant by being a "reflective practitioner."

By *reflecting in action*, you inform your understanding of yourself as a teacher and your children as learners. Your understanding will determine your next steps; the end of one learning experience for you and your students will be the beginning of the next experience. In just a short time, you can develop the *reflection in action* mindset toward teaching.

Utilize a Process (The Five-Step Action Research Process)

Action research can be framed in varying contexts and live under many different names. General Classroom Inquiry, Lesson Study, Teacher Work Sample Methodology, and Response to Intervention (RtI) are a few. Within any of these action research models your work is generally guided by a process, such as depicted in figure 1.2.

- Step 1. Issue Identification
- Step 2. Data Collection
- Step 3. Action Planning
- Step 4. Plan Activation
- Step 5. Outcome Assessment

It is important at the point to have a closer look at each one of the five steps of action research.

Step 1: Issue Identification

Issue identification is generally an initial starting point for your action research. You will find that action research is often used by teachers to solve problems in their classrooms and schools because it is such an excellent problem-solving process. However, you do not necessarily have to have a problem to solve before undertaking an action research project.

By taking an exclusively problem-centered approach, you risk overlooking important opportunities for growth and enhancement. *Issue identification* is a broader, more inclusive term indicating the limitless scope of possibilities you might choose to investigate. Perhaps you are questioning some teaching tradition and you think you can improve upon it, or you seek to better align your teaching strategies with state and local standards. Either of these might be your issue to investigate. Maybe you have heard or read about a great idea and now want to see how this "best practice" fits with your teaching and affects your learning environment. Your "teacher intuitions" and hunches are powerful and valued in the action research process.

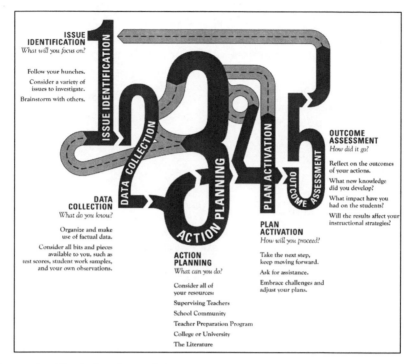

Figure 1.2.   The Action Research Process
Source: **Information Graphic by Amanda Gingery Hostalka © 2010. All rights reserved.**

Consider looking at chapter 2, "Setting the Stage: Understanding the Importance of Context in Action Research," when deciding on an issue to study. This chapter focuses on various factors related to the setting in which your action research study will take place. Carefully studying the circumstances and conditions of the learning environment will help sharpen your awareness of your classroom and your students' needs, helping you pinpoint an issue you'd like to focus on.

Also chapter 3, "Framing Your Action Research Study," will help you take that initial "inquiry hunch" or feeling about what you might want to study and develop it into a well-focused issue to investigate. If you have already decided you are going to do a Lesson Study, Teacher Work Sample Methodology, or Response to Intervention (RtI), be sure to reference *Action Research for Teacher Candidates* (Pelton 2010) for the fundamentals of these approaches.

Step 2: Data Collection
Data is an essential part of action research. Almost anything in your classroom might serve as potential data for your study. It is important to under-

stand that collecting, organizing, and reflecting on your data begin in the initial stages of your action research and continue throughout the entire process. Some common action research data might include the following:

- Anecdotal records
- Student work samples
- Classroom test scores
- Standardized test scores
- Running records
- Homework
- Parental feedback
- Formal and informal observations

Your data will serve to guide you and validate your current actions, as well as to assess the final outcomes of your work.

Step 3: Action Planning

Regardless of the type of action research study you decide to carry out, you will need to create a plan of action. Your plan of action will address the issue you identified in step 1.

When planning your action, you should reflect upon your issue by exploring it in terms of expert input. This is where the culture of collaboration in action research becomes especially important. Think about all the resources available to you when you are developing your action plan: teachers, specialists, college or university professors and clinical supervisors, school administrators, professional literature, and this text are all resources.

Look to chapter 6, "Learning Conversations," and chapter 7, "Tools for Collaboration," for communication strategies to support your work with others. Finally, chapter 8, "Developing an Action Research Communication Plan," needs no explanation. The result of reading and working through chapter 8 will be that you will have a plan for concise communication with all of the stakeholders of your study. The strategies that are provided throughout these chapters focus on communication and planning and will help you craft an effective action plan that addresses the issue you identified in step 1.

Step 4. Plan Activation

The plan activation stage of your action research is where the investment in your preparation really pays off! As you implement your action plan, you can do so with the confidence that you have reviewed data, researched best practices, and developed the best possible plan to meet your students' needs.

As your action research unfolds, remember the *reflection in action* mindset of an action researcher, *action-data-reflection* and more action. Be sure to respond in a way that best serves your students. You might find that you will need to change your plans based on the current data that is generated during this stage. In action research, changing your plan based on data that is being generated is a strength of the process. Simply make the changes, document the effect, and continue to move forward with your study.

Step 5. Outcome Assessment

In step 5 of your action research, you will use all of your data to draw some conclusions about the effectiveness of your work with children. You must also pause to consider the implications of this new knowledge. What will you do with this new information about your teaching and learning environment? How will it impact your growth and development as a teacher? How does it fit within the broader context of the entire school environment?

Along with the many benefits to children, the action research process might uncover a new problem that needs a solution or a new issue that needs to be investigated. Make this an opportunity to continue your work with the mindset and skill sets of an action research–oriented teacher.

Be Flexible to Change

As you have seen from reviewing the five-step action research process, action researchers are often engaged in a series of steps, as shown in figure 1.2. However, the approach is one that does not always need to proceed in a straight line. You will often find yourself looping back to a previous step before moving forward to the next one.

In the Action Planning step, for example, you may find yourself at the threshold of a plan of action. You will soon be making choices and engaging in activities that will address the issue you previously identified in step 1. You have collected data and have started to sort through it. You are reflecting upon its possible meanings for your project. The data has begun to tell you a story about your students. In that stack of papers are clues that answer the next big question: What do I do next? You might think ahead to step 4: Plan Activation.

Your next thought may very well be "I need more information, more data." Excellent! No one expects you to gather your research data and instantly know what to do in the classroom. That is why step 3 is called

Action Planning. During your Action Planning, you will continually inventory your resources and practices to ensure that you are making your best attempt at utilizing the most beneficial strategies. Perhaps, at this point, you may decide to circle back to step 2 and collect more data. Or, maybe your next step is to remember the basic framework of action research; collaboration (which will be further discussed later in this chapter). But don't worry, you are not alone. Get input from others. Continue using your resources and data. Then, use your *reflection in action* mindset to help guide your action plan.

You will discover that the action-data-reflection-action sequence of action research, shown in figure 1.1, cycles and recycles as you proceed within the larger action research process pictured in figure 1.2. Action researchers embrace this flexibility and realize that there is some unpredictability in teaching. We make allowances for the unexpected experiences every educator faces. As mentioned earlier, make changes to your research plan, document those changes, and then continue the process.

Pay Attention to the Data

Paying attention to the data can't be stressed enough! During all stages of your action research your data must guide your study and give direction to your teaching by affirming what is working and indicating what is not. Paying attention to a range of data provides you with multiple points of view on your classroom, which leads to greater accuracy in planning for a change or an enhancement of your teaching practices.

When conducting your action research, it is often difficult to decide which data, or, what type of data—quantitative or qualitative—you should use to guide your work. In short, we have found that using a combination of types of data can usually provide the clearest and most accurate picture of what is happening in your teaching and learning environment. Using both quantitative and qualitative data in a study is referred to as *mixed methods* research design. Although this represents a shift away from focusing on standardized test scores alone to make instructional decisions, action research–oriented teachers believe that having a wealth of information about the teaching and learning environment provides the best vantage point for instructional decision making.

A thorough discussion and examples of mixed methods research is provided in chapter 4, "Qualitative Plus Quantitative: Mixed Methods Research Design." Chapter 4 will guide you on how to capitalize on the synergy of using both types of data to inform your study.

Be creative in the types of data you use to support your research. Because technological devices, such as $100 flip video recorders, are so accessible and easy to use, chapter 5, "Video Studies for Improving Classroom Teaching-Learning Performances," is dedicated entirely to teaching you how to use video studies to support your work as an action researcher.

Finally, remember the action research mindset (figure 1.1) of *reflection in action* (data-reflection-action). Your data serves as the pivot point for effective reflection, which will direct you to your next steps in action research. Paying careful attention to your data is what makes an action researcher truly successful.

Collaborate with Others

As mentioned earlier in this chapter, collaboration can be a very powerful and productive experience for action researchers. Collaborating with others can help you clarify your thoughts during the many stages of the action research process. Those in your immediate learning environment, including your fellow teachers, can make excellent partners in helping you sort through your data and reflect upon your teaching.

At any point during your action research, but particularly during action planning, you should remind yourself to consult with all possible experts in the field. Mentor teachers have years of practical experience and love to help others engage in authentic learning. They generally enjoy sharing their knowledge of teaching and learning. Contact your local college or university professors and ask them about theories and strategies related to your topic.

If you are addressing an issue related to math or reading, for example, be sure to access your school specialists; these teachers represent a wealth of knowledge and can often direct you to resources and materials relating to your issue. Contact the professor who taught your methods courses. Go to these professionals with your current issue, initial data in hand, and discuss what might work best in addressing your specific students' needs. Tap into them! Learn from their examples and borrow from their conventional knowledge. However, be cautious not to just copy what someone else has done or do what someone has told you to do—you may lose the transformative power of the *reflection in action* part of the action research process. Instead, develop *your own* action plan by gleaning information from all your resources. A synthesis of this information will help you begin identifying and shaping your own best practices.

If you know of others who are doing or have done action research, seek them out. Action researchers are collaborative by nature and enjoy helping each other. They embrace a culture of inquiry and will support your work.

When planning your action, in addition to the expert counsel available from those in your teaching environment, make use of the collected wisdom of the academic community found in libraries and computer databases. A review of the literature is an integral part of the discipline of being an action researcher. You will find a growing number of articles published for teachers by teachers. It will be enriching to discover what others have done regarding issues similar to yours.

Librarians generally take a keen interest in students researching topics for practical application and can help make your search more efficient. Formal databases such as ERIC will help you zero in on those educators working on issues similar to yours. Even Internet surfing can turn up a surprising amount of useful material. Professional organizations can provide a tremendous amount of information as well. There is at least one specialized organization for every imaginable area of education.

Use all of your resources to gain knowledge about all the possibilities and then consider how to put these ideas into action for you and your students.

Be a Responsive Teacher

When you implement the action research process, positive changes will occur in your classroom over the course of days, weeks, months, and into the years. However, bringing effective change to your class can also be an immediate process *while* you are teaching. A microcosmic perspective of the action research mindset is to be aware of how your learners are reacting to your immediate instruction, and then take action based upon their needs in the here and now. This is called responsive teaching.

Responsive teaching is about applying the *reflection in action* mindset, moment to moment. Doing so will enable you to differentiate instruction at the appropriate instant, based on the data that flows from the teaching and learning environment. Practicing responsive teaching builds what is probably the most important professional teaching capacity you can have: being able to think on your feet and respond efficiently and effectively *in the moment*. As you take action during these teachable moments, new data will result, affirming the effectiveness of your responsive teaching. At these particular times, you are learning about teaching *while* you are teaching, which can only occur in the field, when working with students. What you are creating is genuine, real-time, data-driven instruction.

Conclusion

This chapter began by posing a simple question often used to begin a class-room inquiry study: *How well are my students learning what I am teaching?* The skills and qualities of an action researcher go a long way in helping you answer that question. But even more importantly, becoming an action research–oriented teacher will also ensure that another question, *How well am I teaching what students need to learn?* is answered. The result: a high-quality teaching and learning environment for you and your students!

Action research is quickly becoming adopted as a method of professional development for inservice teachers and a process for overall school renewal as well. Whether you are a preservice teacher participating in action research for the first time or an inservice teacher with an interest in bringing students the best possible teaching strategies, action research is a perfect curriculum for growth and development. You will find that the strategies provided in this book will help you become an action research–oriented teacher and assist you in meeting—and exceeding—your greatest teaching and learning goals. Now go out and do it!

Questions for Review and Reflection

After you are finished reading and thinking about this chapter, you will be able to:

1. Discuss what it means to be an action research oriented teacher
2. Identify and explain the five-step action research process
3. Describe the role of data in action research

References

Pelton, R. P. (Ed.). 2010. *Action Research for Teacher Candidates: Using Classroom Data to Enhance Instruction.* Lanham, MD: Rowman & Littlefield, 2010.

CHAPTER TWO

∿

Setting the Stage: Understanding the Importance of Context in Action Research

David W. Nicholson

This information helps me understand where the students are coming from.

—Teacher candidate

This chapter focuses on various factors related to the setting in which your action research study will take place and the characteristics of the students you will be studying. These factors establish the *context* of your study, providing you (as the action researcher) with background information that describes the circumstances and conditions of the learning environment.

Describing details of the context helps support the credibility of your action research study's findings, and gives perspective to the conclusions you draw regarding the impact of instruction. Often, important factors that influence learning are hiding in plain sight—meaning that they are present in the setting every day yet remain virtually unseen, and therefore they are not taken into account when undertaking an action research study. Collecting data on context makes the unseen *seen* and sets the stage for your action research study. Context helps you understand the implications of various factors on teaching and learning, and it should not be overlooked or taken for granted as you conduct your study.

By the time you finish reading and thinking about this chapter, you will be able to:

- Identify and recognize the various contextual factors that impact the learning environment
- Collect and analyze data on the school and classroom setting of the action research study
- Collect and analyze data on the characteristics of the students in the setting of the action research study
- Collect and analyze data on the characteristics of the local community of the action research study
- Describe and explain the instructional implications of contextual factors

This chapter will address the following guiding questions:

- How will understanding context benefit my action research study?
- What resources are available for accessing data on the context of my action research study?
- Is my school representative of the school system?
- Is my classroom representative of the school?
- What community factors play a role in the learning environment?
- What are the instructional implications of contextual factors?

This chapter presents a process for collecting information at various levels: (a) school system, (b) school, (c) community, (d) classroom, and (e) students of your action research.

a. *School system* factors include such characteristics as geographic location, size of enrollment, demographics of system and school student population, results of mandated standardized test score reports and Adequate Yearly Progress (AYP), and so on.
b. *School* factors include geographic location, size of enrollment, demographics of system and school student population, results of mandated standardized test score reports and Adequate Yearly Progress (AYP), and so on.
c. *Community* factors include geographic location, population size, demographics of community population, extent of community support for education, degree and kind of parental involvement, and so on.
d. *Classroom* factors include grade level; enrollment; student-teacher ratio; physical features of classroom; availability of and access to technology, library, media, and other resources; availability of and access to student support services; classroom rules and routines; grouping patterns and seating arrangements; scheduling; and so on.

e. *Student* characteristics include age, gender, race/ethnicity, socioeconomic status, achievement levels, developmental levels, exceptional learning needs, cultural background, language, and so on.

The implications of these contextual factors on instruction and assessment should be considered throughout your action research study, to ground the findings in the local setting of the study, relate the immediate context to the broader learning and living community, help justify your conclusions, and assist in formulating recommendations to address the needs discovered. After all, developing a plan of action to implement within the local setting is a primary goal of conducting action research.

Benefits of This Chapter

Guiding Question: *How will understanding context benefit my action research study?* Considered together, the contextual factors described above provide the "big picture" of your study. This broader perspective will help you better understand the setting and the students involved in your action research, and better understand yourself as a teacher candidate and action researcher.

Guides, manuals, handbooks, and textbooks on action research stress the importance of context, not only inside the classroom but also within the school and the outside community (Girod 2002; Johnson 2005; Renaissance Partnership 2002). The credibility of the results you report will be strengthened by describing the factors that influence teaching and learning. This chapter expands upon existing resources by recommending that teacher candidates increase the kinds of data collected, specify and verify the sources of data, analyze and compare data, and interpret data across a wider range of interrelated contextual factors.

More important, the process will encourage you to examine the instructional implications of these contextual factors and how these factors influence instruction and assessment. The perceived impact your study has on student learning is in large part a matter of context, of relating your findings to the conditions and circumstances of the setting and the characteristics of the participants selected to study.

Collecting this data will engage you in professional collaboration. Establishing context requires collaborating with your classroom teacher and other school personnel to gather information.

In discovering context, you will gain knowledge about the community the school serves and the outside-of-school environment in which the students live and develop.

A final benefit is to achieve a greater understanding of yourself as an educator by comparing the context of your own learning experiences to those of your students. Developing professionals need to be willing to reflect on the influences that have impacted their own learning. Research indicates that prior experiences as a student affect a teacher candidate's assumptions, expectations, perceptions, and practices in the classroom (Kagan 1992).

How This Chapter Is Organized

Each section of this chapter guides the reader through the process of collecting data on the setting and students of your action research study. The following topics will be examined:

- Locating and using resources
- Collecting data on contextual factors
  o The school system and placement school
  o Your classroom and students
  o The community
- Instructional implications
- Appendixes
  A. Sample Data Table (Table I)
  B. Elements of Written Consent
  C. Extension Activity: Comparing Your Placement School to the School You Attended as a Student
  D. Online Sources for Locating Data

The chapter begins by discussing sources of data and explains how to locate and use these sources. Each section thereafter provides blank tables (graphic organizers) for recording and organizing data and sources. A sample data table appears in Appendix A to use as a model, providing real data on an actual school system and school—data that can be verified from sources that you can readily access.

Based on the data collected, you will be asked to draw comparisons among (a) the school system, (b) the placement school, and (c) your placement classroom. Based on these comparisons, you will examine and address the implications of specific contextual factors that you believe influence instruction or impact learning.

Throughout the chapter, quotations and findings are reported from my own action research study on contextual factors (Nicholson 2009), information from actual teacher candidates that I collected and analyzed as inquiry into my own instruction and reflection on my own practice as a teacher educator.

Locating and Using Resources

Guiding Question: *What resources are available for accessing data on the context of my action research study?*
A variety of sources exist to furnish the kinds of data you will be expected to collect. Most of the data on the school system and the schools is public information, which should be available to anyone. Some of this information will be accessible at your placement school by request from the school office. However, much of the data on the school system and placement school can be collected exclusively from online, publicly available sources.

Certain information on the classroom and students cannot be located using external sources. In those instances, use sources at your school, such as your supervising teacher, office personnel, the school's strategic plan, the guidance counselor, and so on. Also, some of the information can be based on your own direct observations in the setting.

At no time will you be requesting confidential information that would identify any individual student by name. However, if you or your teacher believe information of a potentially sensitive nature is recommended for collection within a chapter section, suggestions on how to handle those cases will be offered.

Identify the specific sources for all data so your information can be readily accessed and verified by a reader. Cite the source(s) under each data set in the tables (where indicated), rather than in an overall list at the end of the entire action research study report (such as "Works Cited" or "References"). If a reader wishes to verify data as he or she reads your research study, an alphabetical reference list at the end will not indicate with precision exactly where each data item has been retrieved. This will oblige your reader to attempt to reproduce your data search, which will be frustrating, time consuming, and an unnecessary inconvenience. Furthermore, if the reader is unable to locate your data, the credibility of your results is diminished. If you are conducting this action research study for an assignment within your teacher education program, your college or university supervisor or professor may not accept data that does not cite a credible, verifiable source.

Primary data sources are preferred for contextual data. Whenever possible, locate data directly from the school, school system, and/or state and national databases. For example, for data on enrollment, student population demographics, teacher-student ratio, state testing results, and so on, use the school system and/or the state department of education websites as sources. The National Center for Education Statistics (NCES) website (nces.ed.gov/) houses a great deal of information that may prove important to the context of your action research study. A list of suggested websites is provided in appendix D at the end of this chapter. The Sample Data Table (appendix A) displays information collected exclusively from publicly available sources.

Rely on secondary data sources (e.g., from commercial sites such as Public School Review, Great Schools, School Matters, etc.) only when you are unable to locate data from a primary source. In most cases, information on these sites has likely been obtained from primary sources. However, when information cannot be located from a primary source (such as teacher-student ratio), use secondary sources to offer available information to the reader. It is best to search more than one site, as commercial sites may not update their information as frequently as primary sources, and the data may vary. Try to record in your tables the most recent information possible, and provide more than one source if the data do not agree.

Data on community characteristics can be acquired from a variety of free commercial websites (such as MuniNet Guide, City-Data, and ePodunk). These sites provide geographic location, size of community population, socioeconomic profile (using such indicators as median household income or median housing values), median age, gender and ethnicity proportions, and so on. A list of suggested websites is provided in appendix D at the end of this chapter.

The sources reported need to be precise enough for the reader to have direct and ready access to the information. In other words, if you use a school system website to obtain a variety of data (e.g., enrollment figures, demographics of student population, teacher-student ratio, state testing results, etc.), provide a direct link to *each specific page or area* of the website for each data set. If this is not possible, describe in detail the steps to navigate directly from the home page to the data you cite. Simply repeating the home page address for a variety of data will require the reader to search the website for each piece of information, which will be extremely time consuming and, as stated above, in essence require the reader to attempt to replicate your work. All hyperlinks need to be active, and each web address (URL) written out in its entirety.

Another important reason to document the sources of your data is for your own use as a researcher. It is highly frustrating to try to retrace your steps during the course of a research project to hunt down where you located data, especially if you have a question or need to make a change. Creating a data trail for your own purposes is vital. Write down the exact source of each data item as you retrieve it, rather than waiting until near the end of the project and attempting to replicate your steps (which will be time consuming, difficult, and in some cases, nearly impossible).

Collecting Data on Contextual Factors

The School System and Placement School
Guiding Question: *Is my school representative of the school system?*

> *It is fascinating to see how elements such as gender percentage and teacher-student ratio can impact the learning environment and student education, whether it be in the school or the county school system.*

> —Teacher candidate

If your placement school is a public school, data on the school system and the school is assumed to be public information. This information can be obtained through the school board office and the school's office, but all the data presented below can be located online. Check to make sure the data you select for inclusion in this section is the most recent available. Primary sources (as discussed above) are preferred, as commercial sources may not be updated as frequently or be as accurate.

Private schools may not publish all the recommended data. In such cases, a visit to the school's office may result in obtaining most of the information. Private schools are not required to report standardized test scores and student achievement progress according to categories such as ethnicity or special needs. However, many private schools do report student achievement on nationally recognized tests such as the Scholastic Aptitude Test (SAT), the ACT, and other tests used for college admissions. They may also report results on Advanced Placement (AP) tests and other measures.

Figure 2.1, "School System and Placement School," is a graphic organizer for you to use to begin collecting and organizing information so that school system and school data can be directly compared. The cells are divided by a horizontal dashed line. Write the data collected above the dashed line, and the source of that data below the dashed line. Remember to cite specific sources for each data set, sources that can be readily accessed and verified. Refer to the Sample Data Table (appendix A) for an example of a completed table.

Comparison of Placement School to School System
Figure 2.1 offers a convenient means to directly compare the school system to your placement school. Each data type is organized in a row, and you need only compare column A to column B across each row to quickly notice similarities and differences between the school system and the school.

Figure 2.1. Graphic organizer: School system and placement school.

Factors	A. School system Data Source	B. Placement school Data Source
1. Name of school system/school		
2. Geographic location (be specific)		
3. Number of schools		
4. Student population (enrollment number)		
5. Title I • For school system: # Title I schools • For school: Yes/No if school Title I, indicate schoolwide or targeted assistance status (if available)		
6. Demographics of overall student population:		
a. Number and/or percentage by gender		
b. Number and/or percentage by ethnicity		
c. Number and/or percentage special needs services students (e.g., 504, IEP, ESL, gifted and talented, etc.)		
d. Number and/or percentage Free and/or Reduced Meals (FARMS)		
7. Teacher-student ratio		
8. Statewide standardized testing results • Indicate if school system and/or school *met* or *did not meet* state standards/AYP (Adequate Yearly Progress). • If *did not meet,* identify the specific *subject area(s)* and/or *subgroup(s)* and provide that data.		

Using the text box "Similarities between Placement School and School System," identify which school data (column B in figure 2.1) are noticeably similar to the school system data (column A in figure 2.1). Be specific. Note any data that captures your attention (e.g., size of

Figure 2.2. Similarities between placement school and school system.

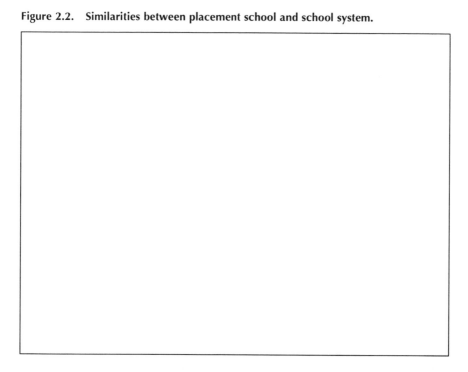

enrollment, gender, ethnicity, special needs, Free and/or Reduced Meals [FARMS], teacher-student ratio, AYP, etc.). This comparison helps answer the question *In what ways is my placement school representative of the overall school system?*

In the next text box, "Differences between Placement School and School System" (figure 2.3), identify which school data (column B in figure 2.1) are noticeably *different* from the school system data (column A in figure 2.1). Be *specific* in your discussion. Note any data that captures your attention (e.g., size of enrollment, gender, ethnicity, special needs, FARMS, teacher-student ratio, AYP, etc.) and helps answer the question *In what ways is my placement school* not *representative of the overall school system?*

Your Classroom and Students
Guiding Question: *Is my classroom representative of the school?*

> *I think that knowing the cultural factors of the students in the classroom is valuable, because as a teacher you are able to get a better understanding of where your students are coming from in their home lives and are able to utilize that knowledge to reach your students on a personal level.*

—Teacher candidate

Figure 2.3. Differences between placement school and school system.

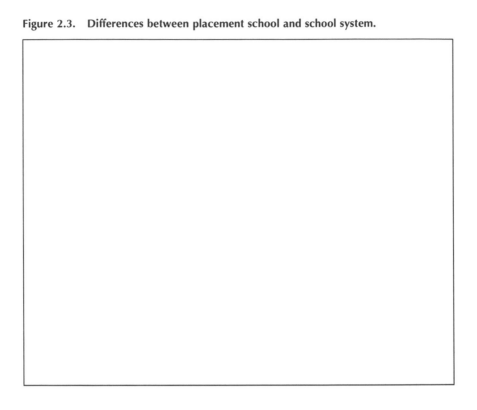

"Your Classroom and Students" (figure 2.4) is a graphic organizer designed to help you compile data on your classroom and the students you teach. As stated in the section above, "Locating and Using Resources," not all of the data on your classroom can be located using external sources. In those instances, use sources at your school, such as your supervising teacher, office personnel, the school's strategic plan, the guidance counselor, etc. In addition, some of the information can be based on your own direct observations. However, you are still required to indicate *sources* of all data (including teachers, staff, your own observations, etc.). The reader must remain confident that your data has been obtained by reliable methods and can be trusted.

Suggestions for Collecting Sensitive Data:
Collecting data on ethnicity, socioeconomic status, and special needs can pose questions or present problems for the action researcher. Public schools are required to report this data to state and federal agencies. Data for these categories for the school system and individual schools can be located online or within documentation available to the public upon re-

Figure 2.4. Graphic organizer: Your classroom and students.

Factor	Data	Source
1. Grade level		
1. Number of students		
2. Gender proportion		
3. Ethnicity proportion		
4. Number and/or percentage special needs services students (e.g., 504, IEP, ESL, Title I, gifted and talented, etc.)		
5. Number and/or percentage Free and/or Reduced Meals (FARMS)		

quest. Nevertheless, the individual teacher in a particular classroom can understandably be uneasy identifying students who meet these criteria to a teacher candidate.

Logic tells us that if the school has the capacity to report the number of students in each of these categories, that this information on students within classrooms does exist in the school. The dilemma is in gaining access. All of this data helps answer the question: *Is my classroom representative of the school?*

The teacher candidate needs to assure the classroom teacher and the school administration that policies regarding anonymity and confidentiality of individual student information will be strictly followed. One way to do this is to have your college or university supervisor meet with you and the classroom teacher and explain the action research process. Bring to this meeting your research proposal and design. An additional safeguard is to furnish the teacher and/or school administration with a written consent form that all parties can sign. (See Appendix B, "Elements of Written Consent.")

Most if not all teacher candidates (especially in internship or student teaching) may already have permission to review student IEPs (Individual Education Plans) and other records pertaining to accommodations and modifications addressing the special learning needs of individual students. Emphasize that you will not in any way identify the individual students, but that you are merely requesting a number or percentage so that you are aware of the contextual factors in this classroom, and to have a number or percentage to compare to the school as a whole and to the overall school system. Bring this handbook to your meeting and allow the teacher and school administrators to see the tables to reassure them of the intended use of this data.

Socioeconomic status is typically reported as students who qualify for FARMS. This information is included in figure 2.1, "Graphic Organizer: School System and Placement School," factor 6d. The school should have this data on record for each student. However, the classroom teacher or school administrator may not wish to, or be in a position to, reveal the number of students who qualify for FARMS at the classroom level. Your request may require the intervention of your college or university supervisor, as part of the meeting that describes your research study.

Ethnicity should also be data the school has collected on each student and has on record. Again, stress that you do not wish to match ethnicity information to any particular student, but to be provided a number, percentage, or proportion of the classroom population. This will serve as a contextual factor and will also be used, as the other data, for comparison purposes. The No Child Left Behind Act (2001) requires states to report school data by categories such as gender, ethnicity, special needs, and socioeconomic status; therefore, this information is legally obtainable and publicly available. Your request is to compare the categories at the school to those at the classroom level, to help determine if your classroom is representative of the overall school profile.

Note: We must exercise great caution in relying upon our own observational skills to identify any given student's ethnicity. Speak to your friends and family, and you will discover a mix of many ethnic backgrounds that cannot be determined merely by visual identification. Therefore, it is best to have the cooperation and support of the classroom teacher, who may have access to formal information from school records. Only as a last resort should any one of us venture to make assumptions about an individual's racial or ethnic background based on visual observation. The same can be said for socioeconomic or special needs status. However, if all other avenues to this data are closed, you can offer general identifications with the explicit caveat that this information is based upon your own observations.

Comparison of Your Classroom to Placement School

The graphic organizer "Your Classroom and Students" (figure 2.4) can be used to directly compare data on your classroom to data on your placement school.

Using figure 2.5, "Similarities between Your Classroom and Placement School," identify which classroom data (figure 2.4) are noticeably similar to the placement school data (figure 2.1, column B). Be *specific*. Note any data that captures your attention (e.g., size of enrollment, gender, ethnicity, special needs, FARMS, teacher-student ratio, AYP, etc.). This comparison helps answer the question: *In what ways is my classroom representative of the overall school?*

Figure 2.5. Similarities between your classroom and placement school.

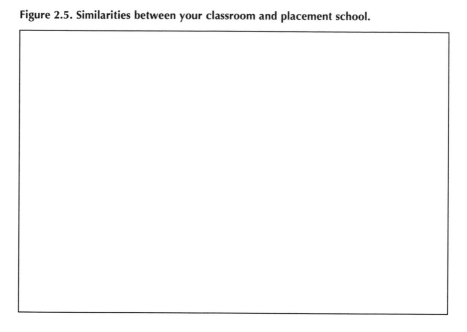

In figure 2.6, "Differences between Your Classroom and Placement School," identify which classroom data (figure 2.4) are noticeably different to the school data (figure 2.1, column B). Be *specific*. Compare any data that captures your attention (e.g., size of enrollment, gender, ethnicity, special needs, FARMS, teacher-student ratio, AYP, etc.). This comparison helps answer the question: *In what ways is my classroom* not *representative of the overall school?*

Facilities and Resources

> I consider the resources that are available within the school to be an extremely valuable factor for understanding the teaching-learning process.
>
> —Teacher candidate

Schools and classroom vary widely regarding the quality and types of facilities and the quantity and availability of resources. These factors are essential components of context. Instruction can be influenced by physical classroom conditions, such as cramped rooms, rooms with too few desks and tables (or broken furniture), underheated rooms in cold weather, stifling rooms in hot weather, bare walls, few or no decorations, noisy heating and cooling units, lack of windows or huge drafty windows (inviting daydreaming and distraction), rooms with dividers that permit sound to carry between classes, and

Figure 2.6. Differences between your classroom and placement school.

so on. Instruction can also be influenced by ample supplies and materials, ready access to current technology, library and media resources, and so on. Resource and support personnel play vital roles in the education of students, and their presence (or absence) can affect student performance.

In figure 2.7, "Physical Features of Your Classroom," describe the general physical features of the classroom, such as the following:

- Classroom size
- Desks/chairs/tables
- Seating arrangements
- Blackboards/whiteboards
- Bulletin boards and decorations
- Furnishings (e.g., rugs, curtains)
- Doors, windows
- Heating units, air conditioning, etc.
- Lighting

You may even wish to sketch a floor plan of the classroom to indicate the existence and location of physical features.

Figure 2.7. Physical features of your classroom.

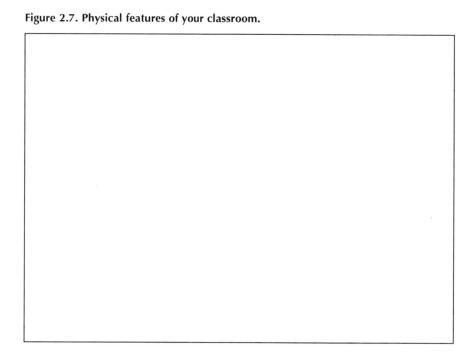

In figure 2.8, "Available Resources," describe the availability of and access of students to the following:

- Resource services (e.g., guidance counselor, school psychologist, special education resource teacher, Title I reading teacher, etc.)
- Library facilities and media resources
- Technology equipment and resources (e.g., equipment available in and/or to classrooms, or to teachers/students, such as computers, LCD projector, TV monitor, VCR/DVD/CD player, computer lab, tech specialist, etc.)

The Community
Guiding Question: *What community factors play a role in the learning environment?*
> *The community where the school is placed is an important factor. Every community is different. It is important for teachers to be able to meet the needs of all students and understand where each student comes from.*

—Teacher candidate

In this section, you will use the graphic organizer in figure 2.9, "The Community," to collect data on the community your placement school serves.

Extending your knowledge of setting beyond the school walls can enrich your understanding of the students and their families and can reveal the level of participation of families in the school and the degree of interaction between the school and the surrounding community.

In addition, your understanding of your role as a teacher candidate can deepen when you become acquainted with the community your school serves and in which the students you teach live. Beliefs and expectations may be reassessed when confronted with a community that differs from our own experience. Often, teacher candidates are unprepared to enter a new, unfamiliar environment, especially one in which the climate differs from one they have previously experienced. Assumptions or impressions brought into this new environment may shape expectations about the students you will be studying for your action research.

On the other hand, if you enter an environment that reminds you of a prior placement or of your own schooling, you may believe that teaching and learning occur in the same manner as in the previous settings. When encountering a community that appears familiar, we may jump to conclusions that may not be entirely accurate or justified. We may assume teachers will instruct in ways we are accustomed to, that students will learn in the same ways we have observed or experienced, that families will respond to the school, teacher, and learning process in a predicable manner. Community factors that impact the school environment can also influence an action research study, affecting how we perceive and interpret data and arrive at conclusions.

Use the "Extended Community" graphic organizer in figure 2.10 to record information on the degree of involvement in the school and/or classroom of parents/guardians, members of the local community, and local organizations and agencies. Student achievement is often correlated with factors situated in the local community, and this information can offer the action researcher valuable perspective. In addition, comparing these factors to your prior experience in previous placements or your own schooling as a student can yield insight into the role the community plays in the learning environment.

Sources of this information may be office staff, administrators, teachers, committees, PTO/PTA, the school system website, the local chamber of commerce, local organizations and agencies that work with the school, and so on.

Instructional Implications

Guiding Question: *What are the instructional implications of contextual factors?*
The data collection you have completed during this chapter culminates with identifying and explaining the implications of contextual factors. Any pre-

Figure 2.9. Graphic organizer: The community.

Factors	Data Source
1. Name of school	
2. Name of community*	
3. Geographic location (be specific)	
4. Demographics of community population	
a. Size of community population	
b. Socioeconomic profile (such as median income)	
c. Median age	
d. Gender numbers and/or percentages	
e. Ethnicity numbers and/or percentages	

* The name of the community can pose questions or present problems. Many schools serve more than one community, communities with a different name from the school's name, and/or communities outside of the immediate vicinity of the school's location. You may need to research more than one community (for example, more than one area/neighborhood name or zip code) to accurately identify communities served by that school.

conceptions you bring to the study, and any conclusions you draw, must be supported by evidence. By completing the activities described in this chapter, you have compiled verifiable data to support assertions regarding the setting of your action research study.

Based on the collected data and your written comparisons, identify and address the instructional implications of specific factors that you believe would impact or influence teaching and learning in your current placement classroom.

Be specific in identifying the factors you are addressing. *Carefully review the data you have gathered in the graphic organizers and text boxes above, and read over the comparisons you have written.* Certain factors will stand out as noticeably different from others, will form a pattern or reveal a trend, will cause you to consider community in a new way, or otherwise prompt you to recognize an important feature about the learning context that you may have overlooked or taken for granted prior to engaging in this process.

Figure 2.10. Graphic organizer: Extended community.

	School	Classroom
5. Parent/guardian and community involvement Data such as: • Number of parents/ guardians attending Back to School Night		
• Visitors for American Education Week • Parents/guardians attending teacher-parent conferences		
• Members of PTA or PTO and number attending meetings • Number attending other schoolwide events		
• Classroom volunteers • Field trip chaperones • Guest speakers from the community		
• Local tax support • Financial or other contributions and donations from businesses or agencies		

Keep in mind that student demographics are not the only factors that may impact instruction. You may choose to discuss facilities, technology, teacher-student ratio, resource services, community demographics—any of the data collected.

Two "factor" text boxes (figures 2.11 and 2.12) have been provided for you to identify and address the instructional implications of selected factors. Of course, feel free to identify as many factors that you regard as important to the context of your action research study and create new boxes to record this data. To get the most out of this exercise, do not merely identify factors, but explain *how* they may impact or influence instruction (e.g., planning, procedures, learning activities, materials, accommodations, assessment, etc.). Moreover, *explain how you will take these factors into account when conducting your action research study, and how these factors may inform the reporting of your findings.*

> Overall, I thought this data collection process was valuable because it gives the teacher candidate a chance to understand the students better.
>
> —Teacher candidate

Figure 2.11. Factor 1.

Figure 2.12. Factor 2.

Conclusion

In my own action research (Nicholson 2009), teacher candidates were asked to rate the value of collecting data on each of the contextual factors described in this chapter. Many differences emerged between the opinions of teacher candidates surveyed prior to conducting action research and the responses of those who had completed action research. As might be expected, standardized test results and Adequate Yearly Progress (AYP) rated highly in both groups. However, the group who had completed action research studies rated factors such as classroom population demographics (e.g., gender, ethnicity, and socioeconomic status) dramatically higher. This latter group rated classroom features, facilities, and resources far higher. Community factors, which were deemed not valuable by candidates prior to conducting action research, rose in the ratings of the group surveyed after completing action research. The importance of contextual factors increased among the teacher candidates who had conducted action research.

This chapter offers you the opportunity to collect data on these important factors *before* you begin your action research, rather than discovering afterward that these factors play a significant role in the setting of your study. Upon completing the activities described in this chapter, the contextual factors you will have investigated and the implications you will have discovered should have a direct impact on your action research study.

These factors should remain in the forefront of your mind, informing and guiding your methods, analysis, and interpretation. It is not uncommon for both preservice and inservice teachers in graduate courses to dutifully identify contextual factors and thoughtfully examine their implications at the beginning of a study, only to subsequently fail to mention them at any other point in their research report. Not to integrate this knowledge throughout your research study is to neglect the value of these factors, to ignore their influence on the setting of your study, and to fail to take action on their relevance. The students you are studying deserve your full attention and respect, and studying the context within which they live and learn helps you better understand and appreciate each of them as unique individuals.

> Overall, I thought collecting context data was valuable because it gives the teacher candidate a chance to understand the students better. I now realize it is important to plan an action research study based on the type of school and its location.
>
> —Teacher candidate

Questions for Review and Reflection

By completing the data tables described in this chapter, you have been able to (a) identify and recognize the various contextual factors that impact learning, and (b) describe and explain the instructional implications of the specific contextual factors you have collected and analyzed. This information will prepare you to conduct your action research study with a solid foundation of background knowledge that can justify your findings and conclusions. You have drawn comparisons between (a) the school and the school system,

(b) the school and your classroom, and (c) the school and the community. These comparisons should enable you to view the overall learning environment with a broader, more inclusive, more holistic perspective.

1. How will collecting data on specific contextual data help me prepare my action research study?
2. Which contextual factors will I continuously keep in mind as I conduct my action research study?
3. What factors differentiate my school from the overall school system?
4. What factors in my classroom are important to understanding the students?
5. How does the local community influence the learning environment?
6. What implications do the contextual factors I have collected and analyzed have on the process of conducting my action research study?
7. What implications do the contextual factors I have collected and analyzed have on the interpretation of the findings of my action research study?
8. What implications do the contextual factors I have collected and analyzed have on the steps for action I will recommend?

Remember to consult the appendixes for a sample data table (appendix A), elements of written consent (appendix B), an extension activity comparing your placement school to the school you attended as a student (appendix C), and a list of online resources for data collection (appendix D).

References

Girod, G. R., ed. 2002. *Connecting teaching and learning: A handbook for teacher educators on teacher work sample methodology*. New York: AACTE.

Johnson, A. P. 2005. *A short guide to action research*. 2nd ed. Boston: Pearson.

Kagan, D. M. 1992. Professional growth among preservice and beginning teachers. *Review of Educational Research* 62 (2): 129–69.

Nicholson, D. W. 2009. Setting the stage: Implications of contextual factors in conducting action research. Paper presented at the Fourteenth Biennial Conference of the International Study Association on Teachers and Teaching (ISATT), University of Lapland, Rovaniemi, Finland, July.

No Child Left Behind Act of 2001, 20 U.S.C. § 6311 et seq.

The Renaissance Partnership for Improving Teacher Quality. 2002. Teacher work sample: Teaching processes prompt and scoring rubric. www.uni.edu/itq/PDF_files/June2002promptandrubric.pdf.

Appendix A: Sample Data Table

TABLE I: School System and Placement School

Factors	A. School system		IB. Placement school	
	Data	Source	Data	Source
1. Name of school system/ school	Baltimore County Public School System (BCPS)	http://www.bcps.org/system/about_us.html	Randallstown Elementary School (RES)	http://randallstownes.bcps.org/
2. Geographic location (be specific)	With a downward wrench-like shape, Baltimore County almost completely extends around the perimeter of Baltimore City. Baltimore County is located north of Baltimore City and Anne Arundel County.	U.S. Census http://quickfacts.census.gov/qfd/maps/maryland_map.html	Randallstown Elementary School is located in the northwest area of Baltimore County.	http://www.bcps.org/schools/boundaries-es-nw.pdf
3. Number of schools	106	2010 Maryland Report Card http://www.mdreportcard.org/rschool.aspx?K=03AAAA		
4. Student population (enrollment number)	103,324 (total school system enrollment)		394 reported on the Randallstown school web site and the 2010 Maryland Report Card. The National Center for Education Statistics (NCES) reported 387 for 2008-2009.	

TABLE I: School System and Placement School

Factors	A. School system		IB. Placement school	
	Data		Data	
	Source		Source	
4. Student population (enrollment number)	2010 Maryland Report Card http://www.mdreportcard.org/Demographics.aspx?K=03AAAA&WDATA=Local+School+System		http://www.bcps.org/schools/profile.aspx?OrgID=22	
			http://www.mdreportcard.org/Demographics.aspx?K=030202&WDATA=School	
			http://nces.ed.gov/ccd/schoolsearch/school_detail.asp?Search=1&InstName=Randallstown+&SchoolType=1&SchoolType=2&SchoolType=3&SchoolType=4&SpecificSchlTypes=all&IncGrade=-1&LoGrade=-1&HiGrade=-1&ID=240012000457	
5. Title I (For school system: # Title I schools) (For school: Yes/No if school Title I, indicate school-wide or targeted status if available)	2009-2010: School-wide 38 Targeted Assistance 6 Total 44 New 2		Targeted A Title I Targeted Assistance Program exists in schools where 35% of students are eligible for Free and/or Reduced Meals (FARMS).	
	http://www.marylandpublicschools.org/MSDE/programs/title1/title1sch/		http://www.marylandpublicschools.org/MSDE/programs/title1/title1sch/	

TABLE I: School System and Placement School

Factors	A. School system		IB. Placement school	
	Data	Source	Data	Source
6. Demographics of overall student population:				
a. Number and/or percentage by gender	The 2010 Maryland Report Card stated that of the enrolled 103,324 students in Baltimore County, 50,540 (or 49%) were female and 52,784 (51%) were male.	http://www.mdreportcard.org/statDisplay. aspx?PV=35|E/M/H|03|AAAA|2|N|7|13|1|2|1|1| 1|1|3	The 2010 Maryland Report Card stated that out of the 394 students enrolled at RES, 204 students (52%) were female and 190 students (48%) were male. The National Center for Education Statistics (NCES) reported 195 (50.4%) male and 192 (49.6%) for 2008-2009.	http://www.mdreportcard.org/statDisplay.aspx? PV=35||03|0202|3|N|6|13|1|2|1|1|1|3 http://nces.ed.gov/ccd/schoolsearch/school_ detail.asp?Search=1&InstName=Randallsto wn+&SchoolType=1&SchoolType=2&Schoo lType=3&SchoolType=4&SpecificSchlTypes =all&IncGrade=-1&LoGrade=-1&HiGrade=- 1&ID=240012000457
b. Number and/or percentage by ethnicity	Out of the total enrollment of 103,324 students in Baltimore County, 647 (.6%) of students were American Indian/Alaskan Native, 6409 (6%)Asian/ Pacific Islands, 41,922 (40.4%) African American, 49,483 (48%) White, and (5%) 4863 Hispanic.		The 2010 Maryland Report Card states that out of the 394 students enrolled at RES, 1 was American Indian/Alaskan Native (.25%), 13 Asian/Pacific Islander students (3.3%), 359 African American students (91%), 13 white students (3.3%) and 8 Hispanic students (.2%).	

TABLE I: School System and Placement School

Factors	A. School system		IB. Placement school	
	Data	Source	Data	Source
b. Number and/or percentage by ethnicity		http://www.mdreportcard.org/statDisplay.aspx?PV=35|E/M/H|03|AAAA|2|N|6|13|1|2|1|1|1|1|3		http://www.mdreportcard.org/statDisplay.aspx?PV=35||03|0202|3|N|6|13|1|2|1|1|1|3
c. Number and/or percentage special needs services students (e.g., 504, IEP, ESL, gifted and talented, etc.)	According to the 2010 Maryland Report Card, 12.7% of elementary students in Baltimore County receive special education services. 2.2% have 504 plans. 36.8% receive Title I services. 6.3% are identified as Limited English Proficient Students.	http://www.mdreportcard.org/StatDisplay.aspx?PV=36:E:03:AAAA:2:N:6:1:1:1:1:1:1:3	According to the 2010 Maryland Report Card, 6.9% of RES students receive special education services. 3.3% have 504 plans. 21% receive Title I services. 5.2% are identified as Limited English Proficient Students.	http://www.mdreportcard.org/statDisplay.aspx?PV=36:E:03:0202:3:N:6:1:1:2:1:1:1:3
d. Number and/or percentage Free and/or Reduced Meals (FARMS)	According to the 2010 Maryland Report Card, 45.4% of students in Baltimore County were eligible for free/reduced meals in school.	http://www.mdreportcard.org/statDisplay.aspx?PV=36|E|03|AAAA|2|N|6|5|1|2|1|1|1|1|3	According to the 2010 Maryland Report Card, 64.1% of RES students were eligible for free/ reduced meals in school.	http://www.mdreportcard.org/statDisplay.aspx?PV=36:E:03:0202:3:N:6:5:1:2:1:1:1:3
7. Teacher:Student Ratio	The National Center for Education Statistics stated the 2009 teacher:student ratio for Baltimore County Public Schools as 1:14.		The Randallstown school website stated average class size as 21.9-23.9. With 25 faculty and 394 students, the teacher:student ratio calculates to 1:15.76. The National Center for Education Statistics stated the 2009 teacher:student ratio for Randallstown Elementary School as 1:16.	

TABLE I: School System and Placement School

Factors	A. School system		IB. Placement school	
	Data	Source	Data	Source
7. Teacher:Student Ratio		http://nces.ed.gov/ccd/districtsearch/district_detail. asp?Search=2&details=1&ID2=2400120&DistrictI D=2400120		http://www.bcps.org/schools/profile. aspx?OrgID=22 http://nces.ed.gov/ccd/schoolsearch/school_ detail.asp?Search=1&InstName=Randallsto wn+&SchoolType=1&SchoolType=2&Schoo lType=3&SchoolType=4&SpecificSchlTypes =all&IncGrade=-1&LoGrade=-1&HiGrade=- 1&ID=240012000457
8. State-wide standardized testing results (Indicate if school system and school MET or DID NOT MEET state standards/ Adequate Yearly Progress (AYP); if DID NOT MEET, identify the specific subject area(s) and/or subgroup(s) and provide that data.)	In 2010, Baltimore County elementary schools met state standards (Adequate Yearly Progress) for reading and math in all applicable areas except special education. 88.6% of elementary students were proficient in reading (special education=73.9%). 86.0% of elementary students were proficient in mathematics (66% special education). 100% of students participated in state standardized tests for reading and math.	http://www.mdreportcard.org/AypGraph.aspx?AypP V=41:1:03:AAAA:2:000000:E	In 2010, Randallstown Elementary School met all state standards (AYP) for reading and math in all applicable areas.	http://www.mdreportcard.org/AypIntro.aspx?Ay pPV=14|0|03|0202|3|000000|A

Appendix B: Elements of Written Consent

For the purposes of an action research study conducted as part of a teacher education program, written consent of the participants is rarely necessary. Research of this nature is typically exempt from the informed consent requirement because the study is conducted in an established or commonly accepted educational setting, involving conventional or routine educational practices (such as instructional strategies), and/or the research collects existing data (such as standardized test results).

The U. S. Department of Health and Human Services (DHHS) publishes policies and regulations governing use of human subjects in research, which can be found at www.dhhs.gov/ohrp/humansubjects/guidance/45cfr46.htm#46.116(c).

Should your teacher education program require informed written consent for action research, the institutional review board of your college or university will have established policies and procedures and will provide the necessary forms. This appendix does not address developing a separate consent form for each individual student in the classroom, signed by a parent or guardian. Your college or university institutional review board would need to approve a study that involves that degree of informed consent.

If your placement school or classroom teacher wishes a written explanation of your research study, you should provide a formal research proposal. However, if the school administration or classroom teacher feels it is necessary to also be furnished with a written agreement that can be signed by both parties, recommended elements of such an agreement are listed below (adapted from the DHHS policies cited above).

Your college or university supervisor will serve as your advisor for developing any written consent form and should sign the document as well. Preferably, the consent will be explained in a meeting attended by you, your college or university supervisor, the classroom teacher, and a school administrator, and the form signed and dated in the presence of all parties.

Basic Elements of Informed Consent for an Action Research Study

1. A simple, descriptive title of the research project
2. Contact information of the researcher (i.e., the teacher candidate) and the college/university supervisor: mailing addresses, e-mail addresses, telephone numbers
3. A statement that the study involves research, an explanation of the purposes of the research, the expected duration of the study, and a description of the procedures to be followed (this should be explained in your research proposal)
4. A description of any reasonable foreseeable risks or discomfort to the subject(s)
5. A description of any benefits to the subject or to others that may reasonably be expected from the research
6. A statement describing the extent, if any, to which confidentiality of records identifying the subject will be maintained
7. A statement that subjects may contact the college/university supervisor at any time during this study if they feel their rights have been violated
8. A statement that participation is voluntary, refusal to participate will involve no penalty or loss of benefits to which the subject is otherwise entitled, and the subject may discontinue participation at any time
9. Signature of the participant indicating consent (such as the school administrator and/or classroom teacher), and the date signed
10. Signature of the researcher (teacher candidate) and the college/university supervisor, and the date signed

Appendix C: Extension Activity: Comparing Your Placement School to the School You Attended as a Student

This extension activity invites you to compare the data you collected on your placement school and classroom to the context of the school *you attended* as a student. This comparison will reveal similarities and differences between the two settings. To view your placement setting with a more informed outlook, think back upon your own schooling, at the grade level you will study in your action research project (e.g., your own elementary school if your action research study is to be conducted in an elementary school). You are not expected to research the demographics and other data of your school as it existed when you attended it. This activity prompts you to comment on any significant similarities and/or differences between the two schools based on your own recollections.

Refer to Appendix A, table I, column IB , which displays the data on your placement school. Based on your recollections of when you attended your school as a student, examine the following factors:

a. In what ways are the placement school population demographics similar to or different from the demographics of the student population of the school you attended as a student?
b. Did your school offer special needs services to students (e.g., learning disabilities, gifted and talented, etc.)?
c. Do you recall students who spoke English as a second language? Do you recall these students receiving any special services?
d. Describe the general physical features of the classroom(s) in your former school (e.g., size, desks/chairs/tables and seating arrangements, blackboards/whiteboards, bulletin boards and decorations, rugs, windows, air conditioning, etc.). In what ways is your current placement classroom similar to or different from the classroom where you learned as a student?
e. Which of the following resources and services were available in your own school and which are available in your placement school?
   - Resource services (e.g., guidance counselor, school psychologist, special education resource teacher, Title I reading teacher, etc.)
   - Library facilities and media resources (describe)
   - Technology equipment and resources (e.g., computers in classroom, projector, VCR/DVD/CD player, computer lab, tech specialist, etc.)

Which of the above factors alter your impression of the learning environment in which you are conducting your action research study? What are the implications of the similarities and differences you perceive?

Appendix D: Online Sources for Locating Data

As stated above in the section "Locating and Using Resources," primary sources are preferred for collecting contextual data. Whenever possible, locate data directly from the school, school system, and/or state and national databases (such as sites ending in .gov). In addition to those sources, below are listed several other websites for locating data. Rely on commercial sites (ending in .com) only when you are unable to locate data from a primary source. Data on community characteristics can be acquired from a variety of free commercial websites, if not available from government sources. When using commercial sites, it is best to compare two or more sites, as the data may vary from site to site.

City-Data.com
www.city-data.com/

Epodunk
www.epodunk.com/

Great Schools
www.greatschools.org/

Muninet Guide
www.muninetguide.com/

National Center of Education Statistics (NCES): Common Core of Data
nces.ed.gov/ccd

No Child Left Behind: State Contacts and Information
www.ed.gov/about/contacts/state/index.html

Public School Review
www.publicschoolreview.com/

School Matters
www.schoolmatters.com/schools.aspx/q/page=fnd

CHAPTER THREE

❧

Framing an Action Research Study

Neal Shambaugh, Jaci Webb-Dempsey, Reagan Curtis, and Rachel Carpenter Heller

"What makes for a good action research topic?" is not an easy question as you learn how to conduct action research. This question deals with issue identification, the first step in the action research model introduced in chapter 1. Your initial choice of action research focus, as mentioned in that chapter, can become a starting point in issue identification. This chapter helps you take that initial hunch or feeling and ask a set of four questions to give your choice a solid foundation.

Choosing an action research topic is frequently based on a new teaching strategy that you find interesting. However, an action research topic should focus first on the learning needs of your students and then on selecting a change in your teaching that helps those students. A good place to start is finding out what the learning priorities in your school are and making sure your action research addresses one of these priorities.

Classroom teachers use many, many strategies during the school day, and it is difficult to pinpoint exactly which one is working. Usually a blend of strategies is what ultimately makes a difference over time. Action research helps you identify student needs and learning outcomes and make a set of teaching decisions to help your students learn.

Chapter Objectives

By the time you finish reading and thinking about this chapter you will be able to do the following:

- Apply a four-question thinking process to help you frame your action research study
- Develop a focus for your action research
- Develop specific research questions based on your focus
- Identify data sources that help you answer your research questions
- Identify the grade-level issues that are inherent in your study

Framing Your Study

Those who have been involved in action research frequently use the term "framing a study" to label this phase of the action research process. Framing a study establishes boundaries to the study. A "bounded" study will be soundly based on students' learning needs and propose procedures that are doable given the limited time you have in your teaching and learning environment. By framing a study you identify who the students are, what the learning challenges and priorities are, and what changes need to occur in your teaching for tomorrow! Thus the use of the word *action* in action research.

A frequently used strategy to prompt student performance is questioning. The use of questioning provides an opportunity for students to explain or demonstrate what they know or don't know. Questioning in some way triggers the human brain to provide answers. This chapter uses four questions to help you frame your action research.

How This Chapter Is Organized

- Four questions to frame action research
- Prompts help you answer these four questions
- Develop an overall research focus
- Develop specific research questions that support this focus
- Identify data sources to answer your research questions
- Grade-level issues to framing an action research study
- Common issues to framing an action research study

The Big Picture: Four Guiding Questions to Frame Action Research

These are the four guiding questions:

1. *Why* do the study?
2. *Who* are the students?
3. *What* are the desired changes in student learning?
4. *How* does my teaching help students learn?

Guiding question 1: *Why* do the study?

Answering the *Why* question forces you to understand the school context in which you work. Your teaching and any action research you conduct *will* be influenced by the realities of this context. Your choice of a topic should address school priorities, specifically the needs of the students in your school.

Guiding question 2: *Who* are the students that might benefit from this action research?

Answering the *Who* question identifies the students' grade level and the content area(s) for your inquiry. Your classroom includes a wonderful range of students, but not all have the same learning characteristics or face the same challenges. These differences in students present challenges for new and experienced teachers alike. One of the benefits of action research is that you will come to know your students better than before. In fact, the long-term value of action research is that it provides a process and a set of habits to continue learning *from* your students over time.

Guiding question 3: *What* are the desired changes in student learning?

Answering the *What* question focuses action research on student learning. This type of action research, sometimes referred to as an intervention study, examines how changes in your teaching practice assist student learning.

While there may be other purposes for action research, this chapter uses student learning to frame your action research. Consider what you have control over. Focus on what you can do in your classroom rather than taking on issues that can affect the whole school. For example, character education or after-school programs would require a significant amount of time to study and might be beyond your current capability.

Guiding question 4: *How* does my teaching help students learn?

Answering this *How* question identifies the changes you are planning to make in your teaching to help your students meet the identified learning outcomes. Generally this teaching change involves the adoption or adjustment of teaching strategies.

Even as a new teacher, you know that no single teaching strategy is sufficient to address all students. For new teachers, the principal focus for action research tends to be whether or not one or more teaching strategies are working. Effective action research, which addresses the reality of classroom

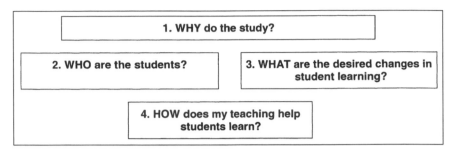

Figure 3.1.   Four Questions to Frame Action Research

teaching, documents how a blend of strategies makes a difference. Figure 3.1 visually summarizes the four questions. This visual strategy is a common approach taken by many teachers to help their students "see" the relationships between concepts or ideas.

Answering the Four Questions to Frame Action Research

Chapter 1 mentioned that the most basic question of education is: *How well are my students learning what I am teaching?* The four questions just introduced will help you be clear about your choice of an action research topic, one that addresses specific student learning needs and specific teaching decisions to help these students. Chapter 1 also explained that action research provides an "organized, proven, and reliable process" to help you in your teaching. This chapter provides another systematic feature to guide you in choosing and framing your action research.

After answering these four guiding questions, you will be able to write specific research questions that frame your study. Once you figure out the research questions, then you can choose the data sources that will help you answer them. To help you answer the four questions, several prompts are provided and are depicted in figure 3.2.

Guiding question 1: *Why* do the study?

Again, your choice of an action research topic is not just about your desire to try out a new teaching strategy. Answering this WHY question helps you mentally negotiate the tension between your teaching interests and school priorities.

To answer question 1:

- Identify the specific student achievement priorities for the school and grade level.

1. WHY do the study?
• Identify the specific student achievement priorities for the school and classroom.
• Summarize the range of student learning needs for that grade level.
• Describe the context that is driving the study, including state, county, school, and classroom/grade level contextual levels.
• Identify any supporting information that may exist.

2. WHO are the students?	3. WHAT are the desired changes in student learning?
• What is the grade level, content area, and/or section to be the focus for your action research.	• Identify the specific learning outcomes desired in those students.
• Describe the developmental differences in your students.	• Connect these outcomes with specific state standards.
• Describe the specific learning challenges.	• Identify incidental learning that could occur.

4. HOW does my teaching help students learn?
• What is the major teaching approach used?
• What are the supporting teaching decisions that need to occur?

Figure 3.2. Answering the Four Questions

- In terms of these student achievement priorities, summarize the range of student learning needs for that grade level. Try to characterize the specific histories and community/family influences that may impact student learning.
- Describe the context that is driving your study. Briefly describe the latest state initiatives, county mandates, and school priorities, and prior attempts to address these priorities (see chapter 1).
- Identify any baseline information on student performance that may exist. This information may be found from individual teachers or official statewide test results.

Guiding question 2: *Who* are the students that might benefit from this action research?

Identify the specific grade level to focus your study on. Decide which content area you are interested in. At the elementary level, your action research might look at a teaching strategy across the entire school day, such as study skill strategies. In this case, your action research addresses study skills across different subjects. Usually, the action research focuses on a specific grade level and content area, such as reading or mathematics. At the secondary level, your action research might involve one or more sections of the same course. We address the question of who will be the students for action research at the end of this chapter.

Answering the grade/content prompt is sufficient for now. After you identify a topic it will be useful to return to this question and answer the second and third supporting items. Developmental differences include cognitive, physical, and social differences common to students at this grade level. Then, record the specific learning challenges experienced by students at this grade level and in this school. This knowledge will come from talking with your supervising teacher and your experience working with this grade level.

To answer question 2:

- Identify the specific grade level, content area, and/or course section that apply to your action research.
- Describe the developmental (cognitive, physical, and social) differences in your students.
- Describe the specific learning challenges faced by your students at this grade level and in this content area.

Guiding question 3: *What* are the desired changes in student learning?

The answer to question 3 will specify what students need to learn. The term *learning outcomes* is used here to characterize improvements in student learning. In terms of the classroom and student priorities you have identified, what changes do you and fellow teachers want to see in students? What knowledge, skills, or attitudes do your students need to learn? Changes in your teaching may also contribute to other forms of learning, such as developing character, behavior, or the self-awareness of one's learning. Are these outcomes necessary? If so, you should record them and be thinking about ways to assess them in your teaching.

Being clear about student learning outcomes is a necessity when you teach any activity, lesson, or unit. Your specified learning outcomes can now be connected to your state standards. Being clear about learning outcomes and connecting these to state standards in your action research demonstrates how you are accountable to state standards and local school priorities.

To answer question 3:

- Identify the specific learning outcomes desired in the students.
- Connect these outcomes to state standards.
- Consider what other forms of learning might occur.

Guiding Question 4: *How* does my teaching help students learn?

Finally, question 4 addresses the teaching question. Initially, you can think about the major teaching strategy that you will use in your action research. For example, you may want to know if having students help each other (e.g., peer learning) makes a difference in helping them solve mathematical word problems. Of course, you realize that good teaching usually requires multiple strategies to reach different students. So your action research is about how different cooperative learning strategies may be used.

Now, list the other teaching decisions that will be necessary to support the major teaching strategy you have chosen. These changes can be organized by recording changes in the overall learning environment, classroom management (e.g., room organization, materials, behavioral policies, procedures, and routines), use of time, teacher activity and student activity, and including how assessment is accomplished in these activities.

To answer question 4:

- What is the major teaching approach you will be using?
- Describe the changes to be implemented to support this teaching strategy. Organize your changes in terms of the categories suggested below:
  - Learning environment
  - Classroom management
  - Time
  - Teacher activity
  - Student activity

To summarize, these four questions help you describe the complex setting that is the public school classroom, identify a full range of student characteristics, specify learning outcomes, and select multiple appropriate teaching strategies and their supporting assessments. Thinking through these questions will help you select a topic for action research—one that is directly connected to student learning and is also interesting for you to study.

Once you have established the purpose for your action research by answering question 1, you can begin to see an overall focus. Answering questions 2, 3, and 4 frames your action research study in terms of this research focus.

Example

An example will be helpful to demonstrate how this is done (see figure 3.3). In this example, you have been placed in a third-grade classroom (question 2). Results of state testing revealed a shortcoming in math test scores, and the principal has directed teachers to work on improving these scores (question 3). In a meeting with the three third-grade teachers, one of the problem areas was that of mathematical word problems and the difficulties third graders have had in applying their math concepts to word problems.

Your mentoring teacher will work with you on developing this study, while the other third-grade teachers have agreed to implement the same study in their classrooms. In this way, all four of you will learn how to conduct teacher research, and more importantly, how changes in teaching will occur differently in the three classrooms.

For question 3, the third-grade teachers have identified word problems as a focus for the action research. Because the strategy of using peer learning has been proposed, the teachers realize that students working together is also an important learning outcome. So in addition to solving word problems, you can

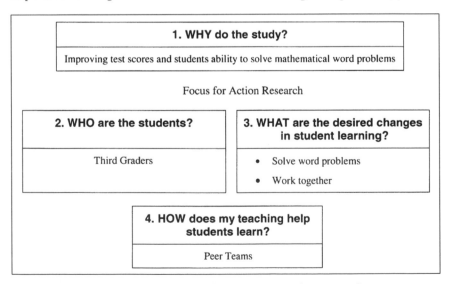

Figure 3.3. Examples Using Four Questions to Frame Action Research

add social learning to the list of learning outcomes. Specifically, the outcome is about helping students learn that they can work together in solving these word problems. In the discussions about the action research topic, teachers voice the possibility that group problem solving may be useful in other content areas. One teacher discusses her concern that student behavior will need to be addressed as students move out from their rows to conduct cooperative group activities.

Finally, for question 4, you bring up the idea of allowing students to work in teams, to learn from each other. The third-grade teachers have identified peer student teams as the primary change in teaching practice, although the question was raised about using other forms of cooperative learning. From the discussions on student behavior, the teachers realize that students will need lessons and practice in working together and setting up appropriate classroom management policies and procedures.

Action Research Focus

Now it is time to frame an action research focus. The way to do this is to combine the answers to questions 2, 3, and 4 in one sentence. So for our example, an action research focus would read as follow:

How do peer teams (How) help third-grade students (Who) solve mathematical word problems (What)?

Now you have a focus for your action research. Thus, the overall structure to framing a research focus takes the following form:

How does X *teaching strategy/change in teaching practice* help Y *students* achieve Z *learning outcomes?*

A summary of this approach is depicted in figure 3.4.

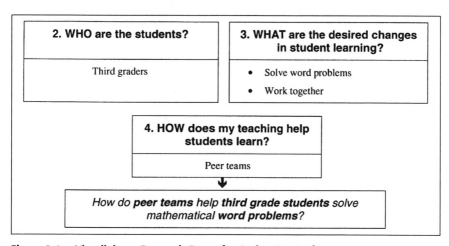

Figure 3.4. **Visualizing a Research Focus for Action Research**

Achieving a research focus is a major accomplishment and benchmark in conducting action research. Now you can take this direction and determine research questions. With research questions you can determine sources of data to answer these questions! Data collection is the second step in the action research model presented in chapter 1.

Framing Specific Action Research Questions and Data Sources

Research Focus and Data Sources

For some teachers, the overall research focus may turn out to be the research question! The next question you should ask yourself is *Can I answer this question?* Answering a research question involves analyzing sources of evidence, which we call data sources. A long-standing view is that data consists solely of numbers. Data sources can include the same tools you used to assess students as before, such as observations, tests, and student work. You can view assessments the same as data sources. The range of assessments, as you will come to realize, may also involve existing data on student performance. Existing data usually involves numbers such as scores on quizzes, test scores, or reading assessments. But existing data might include past student work, such as writing samples, math problems, project artifacts, or portfolios of student-created materials.

Bringing a Research Focus into Research Questions

It is frequently helpful to identify several research questions that support your overall focus. Why? The choice of research questions will greatly ease your choice of data sources to answer these questions, as you will soon see.

Let us continue the use of our word problem example. In your teacher meetings, one of the challenges third graders face involves *selecting relevant information* from a word problem and ignoring the nonrelevant information. A second challenge is coming up with a *procedure* to solve the problem and to *use mathematical operations*. You can now write a research question to address each issue and then think about one or more data sources that together help you answer each of the questions. Refer to figure 3.5 as we go. You reminded the other teachers that you want to find out whether *students can actually help each other* in identifying information in a word problem and then solve it. You can specify this as a third research question and then select one or more sources of data.

See how the above italicized challenges show up in the following three research questions:

Figure 3.5. Identifying Data Sources to Answer Research Questions

How do **peer teams** help **third grade students** solve mathematical **word problems?**

RQ1: How do peer teams help students to identify relevant problem solving information?
- **Data sources:** observation checklist, teacher journal

RQ2: How do peer teams help students to identify problem-solving approaches and use mathematical operations?
- **Data sources:** observation checklist, math journals: problem solving procedures, prompting questions

RQ3: How do peer teams work together and learn from each other during word problem activities?
- **Data sources:** teacher observation checklist, teacher questions on teams

---

> **RQ1:** How do peer teams help students *identify relevant problem-solving information?*
>
> **RQ2:** How do peer teams help students *identify problem-solving approaches* and *use mathematical operations?*
>
> **RQ3:** How do peer teams *work together and learn from each* other during word problem activities?

Identifying Data Sources to Answer Research Questions

Now that you have research questions, the issue of data sources becomes relatively easy. Figure 3.5 records the data sources to answer each of these three research questions.

Research Question 1

Because you are using peer teaching/learning, a key source of assessment is through observation. To capture your observations, a *teacher observation checklist* is developed. A checklist provides a means to record what you remember during classroom teaching. Sometimes a *teacher journal* is used to record these observations, as well as other important memories of teaching. What will you be looking for in the observations to answer each of the research questions?

During your discussions with the other teachers you decide to have peer problem-solving teams made up of three students. Your aim is to mix student abilities and personalities. Each of you then develops observation items for what to look for in terms of identifying (1) relevant information in a word problem, (2) problem-solving approaches and mathematical operations, and (3) group behavior. What you now have is one data source that helps you answer research questions 1, 2, and 3. Again, refer to figure 3.5.

Research Question 2
You mention the use of math journals in which students record their work and respond to teacher prompts. Thus, student math journals become a second data source. The math journals assess students' choice of problem-solving approaches and math operations. The math journal can have students record their responses to your questions about their decisions.

Prompts such as these help reveal students' metacognitive abilities—how they become more self-aware of what they know and don't know and how they learn. Student work samples, such as these math journals, provide key sources of data in action research.

Research Question 3
An observation checklist records your observations of how students work with each other and how they talk about math. A checklist enables you to record observations on a regular basis. Include a space for comments, which can help you make teaching adjustments as well as make sense of (i.e., analyze) the observation checklist data. As a prompt to you, add a space asking yourself this question: "What class and individual adjustments do I need to make?" This question prompts you to take action in your teaching tomorrow.

You can also ask students about their problem-solving approaches and working in a team. Ask them these questions in their groups and hear what they say, and have them record their thoughts in their math journals. You get two ways of assessing what your students are thinking, both in the classroom and more reflective comments. You can begin to see that students' writing ability is also coming into play and could be itself a learning outcome for assessment, particularly if writing across the curriculum is a priority in your school.

Multiple Teaching Strategies = Triangulation
Breaking up your research focus into supporting questions not only helps you identify data sources but also reveals in your action research proposal the full range of your teaching decisions, including classroom management and assessment. Some beginning action researchers choose an action research study that is about the use of math journals, while in our example, the action research study involved math journals and observation checklists as data sources. The focus is on helping these students solve word problems, and math journals is but one teaching decision. The use of student pairs is another.

As you use different forms of assessment to inform you and your students as to their learning progress, the use of these assessments, particularly student work samples, provides different sources of evidence to answer your research question. In research this approach of using multiple data sources is called *tri-*

angulation. You are approaching your research question from different angles and improving the trustworthiness of your conclusions.

Summary
Answering four questions about your action research study helps you frame an overall research focus, develop supporting research questions, and select data sources to answer those questions!

Framing Issues across Grade Levels

This section addresses some of the issues on framing an action research study that differ across grade levels. Action research examples are provided in figures 3.6, 3.7, 3.8, and 3.9, at the end of each section.

Early Childhood Framing Issues
The preschool grade level tends to be a child-centered focus to the curriculum rather than subjects. Teaching at this grade level introduces children to taking responsibility for their behavior within the social setting of the public school and frequently addresses issues of parental attachment—being away from the comfort of family and the home. Another major area is emergent literacy and ways to establish letter recognition, writing, and personal expression. The teacher might spend a great deal of time developing and managing structured play activities. Assessment is primarily through observation. Data sources might include observation checklists or summaries of what students do in addition to the actual student work. Figure 3.6 illustrates a variety of early childhood framing questions.

The choice of an action research topic in preschool depends to a great extent on the suggestions from your supervising teacher involving specific student learning needs. The tendency is to choose a topic based on a teaching strategy, particularly at the preschool level where structured play keys on student activities. The choice of a change in teaching practice should, therefore, involve the use of multiple strategies. There is also the tendency to focus on one strategy and try to prove that this strategy is superior to others or to what the supervising teacher has done. Multiple strategies are always at play here. This choice will be discussed later in the next major section on general framing issues.

Elementary Grades Framing Issues
Elementary grades generally consists of kindergarten through fifth grade. Sometimes teachers organize for planning in terms of individual grade levels

Figure 3.6. Early Childhood Framing Questions

Action Research Focus/Questions	Study Challenges
Q1: Does the use of a visual model in vocabulary instruction help students to comprehend basic spatial concept words? Q2: Does this strategy help to increase frequency of these words in students' oral vocabulary? Q3: Does this strategy increase student engagement during vocabulary instruction?	Understanding students' developmental and learning challenges. 7-week study involving teaching 12 spatial concepts. Observation checklists and teacher journal notes are needed as observation is the assessment method.
How effective is puppetry in teaching preschool students strategies for conflict resolution?	Example of a study with multiple data sources: teacher journal, tally checklist, role play activity chart, student survey.
How does nonverbal communication impact student behavior?	This study involved a teacher candidate placement in both preschool and kindergarten. Cooperation of supervising teacher was necessary to gather data.

or professional development in pairs, such as K–1, 2–3, and 4–5. Kindergarten classrooms, while still child-centered much like preschool, have become increasingly subject-area focused. Those children who enter public school directly into kindergarten without preschool present the teacher with more challenges than those who have had preschool.

While elementary teachers tend to teach across all subject levels, beginning action researchers tend to focus on specific content area outcomes, such as math operations or story comprehension. In these grades, behavior remains an explicit learning outcome. Behavior is part of the "content" to be learned in an elementary grade classroom. Socialization with other children and within the school is always part of the school curriculum. In addition, children begin to see reading and behavioral experts assist the teacher in the classroom. Figure 3.7 illustrates a variety of elementary education framing questions.

Action research should be connected with your school's improvement plan. A school priority may be connected with federal or state mandates. One example is Response to Intervention (RtI), a way to identify student learning challenges and then respond at different instructional intervention levels, moving generally from whole-class instruction to groups and then to one-on-one interventions. Action research involving RtI would involve how teaching strategies were used to address student needs, such as reading or mathematics. RtI becomes a broad structure to organize interventions. Another broad approach might be the use of schoolwide themes and using interdisciplinary activities to cover multiple state standards. Action research could then be used to document how your teaching practice achieved these standards in your classroom.

Teachers in the elementary levels use many teaching strategies during the school day, while teachers at the upper grades tend to adopt a few overall teaching strategies, such as direct instruction, discussion, or cooperative learning. General-purpose strategies for elementary grades include the use of learning stations, groups, and the use of technology.

Middle Grades Framing Issues

Action research across the middle school grades, which can vary in public schools to include grades 5–9, provides unique opportunities to document changes in student learning and performance and to better understand students in this developmental stage. Students in these grades seek a greater sense of their own identity and become more concerned with the social setting of the middle school, while at the same time coming to understand their place in the larger world. One of the keys to engaging students in the middle grades is to take advantage of their desire to be autonomous and social through hands-on activities that are related to their new interests.

Learning for middle school students shifts from the single elementary classroom to different rooms with specific content and subject area focus. Action research at the middle school grades takes on some of the same issues as for secondary grades, such as conducting a study in a specific content area and section. Research questions might be formulated that key in on behavioral and affective learning, such as the appreciation of literature, the valuing of different cultures, and the understanding of the complexity of the physical world and the living world.

Teaching strategies at the middle and secondary grade levels can be general teaching model approaches or they can involve content-specific teaching strategies. General teaching approaches can include direct instruction (DI), which features guided and individual practice. Inductive learning, in which students develop their own category system to understand topics and concepts, is an example of a cognitive strategy useful in reading (e.g., text predictions) and writing (e.g., organizing details and big ideas). Another type of teaching model focuses on inquiry and can be used not only in science but also in mathematics, social studies, reading, and writing. Social teaching models, such as cooperative learning, include a range of strategies from jigsaw and think-pair-share to work teams; they can be useful across all subjects, helping students learn concepts and problem-solving skills, but also working in groups. Figure 3.8 illustrates a variety of middle school education framing questions.

Figure 3.7. Elementary Education Framing Questions

Action Research Focus/Questions	Study Challenges
[K] Research Focus: How does prediction improve kindergarteners responses to oral comprehension questions after a read aloud? Q1: Which comprehension features do students use to recall setting, characters or main events? Q2: Which books support the students' ability to recall setting, characters and main events?	6 students Action researcher: *"Although my primary source of data collection was the story checklists, I was aware that having only one source of data would not in itself be sufficient to yield accurate and reliable results in my study; therefore, I also used four additional sources to collect and analyze data."*
[2nd grade] Q1; How great is the effect of retell activities in relation to reading comprehension? Q2: Will oral strategies increase students' comprehension abilities more than written retell strategies?	Q1 could be improved: "To what extent do retell activities improve 2nd grade learning comprehension. Inconclusive results suggest an improvement in teaching, as here where the action researcher reported the need in her 12 week study to add oral assessment to the written assessment.
[4th grade] Q1: Would implementing Literature Circles keep above-level readers on task during guided reading group with minimal teacher-guided instruction? Q2: Would the students be able to discuss story elements among themselves? Q3: Would the students be able to discuss ways in which they could relate the text to themselves and the text to another text? Q4 Would Literature Circle activities promote discussion of story elements and relating of text to self and text to text in student writing or reports?	Yes/No questions could be changed to "how" questions. Example of a belief in the teaching strategy, despite the findings of this study, which were inconclusive. Sometimes an action research study reveals incidental learning occurs, such as "sense of community" in this study.
[4-5th] Q1: What effect will the integration of the arts have on students' attitudes towards social studies? Q2: What effect will the integration of the arts have on the test scores of the students? Q3: What effect will collaboration have on teaching?	Example of a broad teaching approach (arts integration) on a content area, and the overall interest of the researchers on teaching to the whole student, a broader view of teaching in action research. Two teacher candidates exploring how arts integration impacted students at two different schools. Teacher candidate: *"We plan to present this material to other teachers in hopes of continuing professional development and spreading enthusiasm for arts integration. To continue our voyage in becoming life-long learners, we wish to complete a longitudinal study based on our implementation and findings."*

Figure 3.8. Middle School Education Framing Questions

Action Research Focus/Questions	Study Challenges
[8th MATH] Q1: Does the implementation of daily word problems for a warm up exercise increase student achievement? Q2: Does student confidence increase with daily word problem practice?"	Conducted across multiple middle school math section. Inclusive setting included students with special needs. Attitude surveys used to find out about student confidence.
[6th LANGUAGE ARTS] Q1: If students were more involved in the assessment process and understood better how they would be graded, would they be more motivated to do well? Q2: Could grades increase because of the added knowledge and motivation? Q3: Would added knowledge of assessment through grading rubrics give students more ownership of their assessment outcomes?	These Yes/No questions could be changed to "how" questions. 6-week study in 4 different classrooms
[6th grade MATH] What is the effect of the use of a graphic organizer during math instruction combined with repeated practice on accuracy and fluency of single digit multiplication facts for sixth grade students?	We discourage the use of the word "effect" as it is a "research" word and suggest the use of "how does..." Multiple data sources are helpful to provide different ways to answer a research question, as in this case, which included pre/post test, weekly quizzes, student journal prompts, and research journal.

Teaching strategies may also be content-specific, such as the use of concept maps and problem-based learning (PBL) for science, debates for social studies, and reading prompts useful in all content areas. Action research may involve specific topics within a content area or topics identified by other classroom teachers as being challenging for students. Examples of such topics could be specific mathematical concepts, such as fractions; science topics, such as electricity or biological systems; or specific types of writing, such as persuasive or essays. Study skills strategies may be useful topics for action research in the middle school to help these students develop a metacognitive awareness of how they learn. Technology use may become routine in the middle school classroom, as technology use becomes central in the lives of these students. Computers may be a central feature in the classroom, and they may also be used in lab settings.

Secondary Grades Framing Issues

Action research in the secondary grades (9–12) also centers on individual subjects, as teachers generally teach in one specific content area. The choice for action research will be in a particular grade level and section focusing on a specific content-area topic. Action research can also be conducted across multiple sections, but it might be easier to learn how to conduct action research within a specific section and specific intervention. Action research might be involved in mixed-ability classes or low-achieving sections that would benefit from the inquiry.

Action research in the secondary grades may involve the learning of mathematical, scientific, psychological, and social concepts. Learning outcomes also develop skills such as writing persuasive essays, understanding different genres of literature, the use of the scientific method, web page design, or physical coordination. Integrated forms of outcomes may involve the understanding and appreciation of literature, and the development of writing skills and applying those skills in different forms of writing. Outcomes may also include working in teams and problem solving. The priority for action research is identifying student needs before thinking about the change in teaching practice.

To address these learning outcomes, you might choose a specific teaching strategy, such as the writing process, as a means to help students develop writing skills. You might use different forms of cooperative learning or involve numerous types of games. Which games help which students learn which knowledge or skills? Another example would be the development of study skills.

As we know that each student learns differently, an action research study might involve a range of study skills strategies, such as note-taking formats. Action research might also involve a broad category of teaching practice, such as problem-based learning (PBL). Another strategy decision would be the use of portfolios to assess the changes in student learning (developmental portfolio) or provide a way for students to demonstrate their best work across a unit or part of the school year (showcase portfolio). Technology use may also become a routine teaching strategy and a central feature of the secondary classroom. Action research could study the use of technology as a complementary strategy, rather than seeing if a technological approach is better than a traditional approach.

Classroom management issues remain a part of an action research study because they form part of the teaching decisions. Organization of materials and overall policies, rules, and procedures are just as important for the secondary teacher as for the elementary teacher. At the secondary level, the structure of the learning task or activity becomes a critical teaching decision (particularly with PBL)—explaining the rationale and relevance of the task, structuring the activity to provide clear directions, and providing clear

Figure 3.9. Secondary School Education Framing Questions

Action Research Focus/Questions	Study Challenges
[12th grade civics] Q1; Will civic literacy writing assignments increase my student's knowledge of civic issues? Q2: Will students become more informed and involved with what is going on in the world around them? Q3: Will writing on topics that the students themselves select help them to become more engaged in classroom and in current news stories that are discussed in class?	Again, changing the questions from Yes/No to "how" frames the study to reveal the "ways" in which a strategy impacts students. Example of learning that takes place over time, such as attitudes.
[SPANISH II, III] Focus: Will teaching Spanish learners using an input processing approach and teaching the students effective comprehension strategies raise student test scores? Supporting questions: Q1: Will teaching students effective comprehension strategies for Spanish also increase student engagement during whole-class instruction? Q2: Will teaching students effective comprehension strategies for Spanish increase comprehension during class activities? Q3: Will teaching students effective comprehension strategies for Spanish increase participation of homework assignments?	Example of how supporting questions enables an overall research focus to be addressed. Action researcher: *"Doing action research has taught me more than I could have ever learned reading a book or sitting in a classroom. I was able to take into my own hands what I wanted to know from my classroom and my students. I was able to figure out what I knew very well about teaching and some things I need to work on about researching in the classroom and about teaching. My research indicated that using the input processing approach can be beneficial because all students seem to move at the same rate of achievement when instructional strategies are varied to provide for different learning styles."*
[11-12th BIOLOGY] Is there a correlation between the implementation of weekly quizzes and the academic performance of high school anatomy students?	10 week study Results of this study, which were mixed, pointed toward the issue of students' attitude for a future study.

expectations for performance and clear criteria for assessment. The use of homework, for example, involving outside reading and practice, must be accompanied by consequences in the assessment plan.

Special Education Framing Issues

The focus of action research for the new special education teacher may involve how different forms of formal and informal assessment help the special education teacher and general education teacher understand individual

Figure 3.10. Special Education Framing Questions

Action Research Focus/Questions	Study Challenges
[1st, 2nd, 3rd Resource Room] How can interactive stations help a group of special needs students with reading comprehension?	Deciding what the learning stations' features should be and not making them overly complex.
[5th Resource Room] RQ1: What type of graphic organizers do students with learning disabilities have the most success? RQ2: Which graphic organizers did students with learning disabilities like the most and feel most confident using?	3 students The action researcher learned from this action research that other factors can impact students' learning than a single strategy.
[3rd] What effect will the use of the SPELLER strategy have on 3rd grade students with learning disabilities?"	4 students with learning disabilities 6 weeks with 3 weeks traditional spelling strategy (memorization) and 3 weeks new strategy using picture cards, testing, auditory reinforcement. Supporting questions for many action research studies includes (a) learning and (b) student attitudes about the strategy.

students. Action research could be used to study how instructional interventions support a student's Individualized Education Plan (IEP). Action research could be used to study the different uses of assistive technology.

As opposed to action research in general education classrooms where all students are part of the research, special education teaching may include one-on-one with a small number of students. Action research might then address individual cases. Another possibility is co-teaching with the general education teacher, where all students are part of the study but individual cases might be described along with the entire class. In an elementary special education classroom, the action research might look similar to preschool action research, such as emergent literacy, social skills, and appropriate behavior.

Framing Issues Common to All Studies

This section addresses some of the common questions that beginning action researchers have for all studies.

Number of Students in a Study
Who should be a part of the study?
A long-standing view of "research" is the use of a control group in which that group of students or that class would receive one form of instruction

and another section or class would receive the new teaching. However, if you stop to think about this, giving one set of students one approach while giving another set of students a different approach poses some ethical questions. All students should receive the change in teaching practice. All students receive the same teaching, and one documents results by establishing where students start (a baseline of performance determined at the beginning the study) and seeing how students develop or progress over the length of the change in teaching practice, intervention, or use of one or more strategies.

While you implement changes in your teaching for *all* students, case studies of representative students are sometimes used in action research. Sampling students is a strategy to simplify your action research, which is helpful, particularly if you are new to the approach.

Length of Study
How long should I do the study?
A practical issue is determining when and how long a study should take place (this is a major concern for teacher candidates who are given responsibility for the classroom during a placement). Teacher candidates may be given increasing responsibility over several weeks. Baseline data can be gathered early in the school year to give you a starting point for student performance. As a preservice teacher is given more teaching time, you can implement a strategy. During this ramping up, you should orient yourself to the students and the new approach, such as grouping, learning stations, or PBL. In this way, students learn the specific rules and procedures for behavior and performance. New approaches may take some time to implement, particularly if the students are used to a specific approach.

Teachers who have completed action research have said that they now know "how to do action research." They frequently report that their strategy needed more time. Of greatest concern is generally the results. Your results, however, may be minimal or nonexistent. This may be due in part to the short time frame using the new teaching practice. Remember, your choice of strategies is a teaching decision based on what you as a teacher believe should be done for the benefit of students. Your informal and formal assessments of student progress provide the basis for change or moving on. A study of one to two weeks may not tell you much more than "this is what happened."

A study of at least five to six weeks is a general guideline, but this depends on how much time you have to implement your action plan, the complexity of the study, and the nature of the learning. If your action research is about developing skills, more time may be needed to learn basic skills and to apply these skills. If your action research involves higher-order thinking, your students may need some weeks to develop this thinking and apply knowledge and skills. Frequently, higher-order thinking involves a level of attitude and appreciation. If your action research involves students' valuing something or coming to internalize a belief, such development will take time. Is your action research long enough to document such change, or do you need to think about making initial steps towards this performance?

Teaching Strategies
Is there a more effective teaching strategy than another?
Action research tries to help a teacher answer this question. However, action research is not about proving one strategy works better than another. Why? While this can be demonstrated in some studies, it is very difficult to prove that one strategy has finally been discovered to help students learn fractions, for example.

One of the things you will learn from conducting action research is being able to explain better than before the extent to which your teaching helped your students. Thus, action research is seen by some states and principals as one way to document teacher accountability. In the past, you may have had an overall sense of student performance based on observations or student work. The action research activity forces you to base your conclusions on actual data and to make sense of this data in ways you have not done before. Another term you might hear is *data-driven decision-making*. Action research is one way to accomplish this.

Action research can also document how the use of different strategies helps one type of student over another type or how different strategies might be more effective with specific concepts or skills. An example here is the use of note-taking strategies. A study might involve the use of different ways to take notes and see which note-taking strategy helps the students. With older students you can actually ask them about the effectiveness of the strategies, prompt them to think out loud about their use, and ask them to make suggestions for their future. Such a study is not about finding the one note-taking strategy but perhaps finding that X strategy works best for Y student about Z topic or idea.

Chapter Wrap-Up

Big Ideas of This Chapter
- To help with issue identification, the first step in the action research model, work through the four questions addressing issues of

action research purpose, students, learning outcomes, and teaching changes to help you frame an action research study into an overall research focus.

- Determine if additional research questions are needed.
- Identify sources of evidence to answer each research question.
- Teaching involves a blend of teaching strategies. Your action research study should tell the story of how your teaching practice needed to change to meet students' learning needs.

Immediate Benefits from This Chapter
- It keeps student learning in the forefront of your study.
- Answering the four questions enables you to frame a research focus and specific research questions.
- With specific research questions, you can determine data sources to answer those questions.
- You now have direct evidence to adjust tomorrow's teaching as well as to answer research questions.

Long-Term Benefits from This Chapter
- You and your supervising teacher gain experience in data-driven decision-making.
- Action research results provide a school with a localized knowledge base to build over time, as many student learning priorities require ongoing attention and replication studies may be needed.
- Some content areas, such as second language, may not be assessed by states, and action research provides a way to hold you accountable for your teaching in this area.

Questions for Review and Reflection

1. Adapt the four-question process discussed in this chapter to action research that involves a focus other than teaching intervention.
2. Which of the four questions do you know the least about? How will this level of awareness influence how you frame a study? What changes will you need to make?
3. Describe the likelihood that your study proposal might change. Discuss this possibility with your teacher.
4. What are your perceptions on the range of data sources you will use to answer your research questions?

5. What are some of the tensions and challenges that you have experienced so far with choosing an action research study? Share these issues with your peers.

CHAPTER FOUR

Qualitative plus Quantitative Data: A Mixed Methods Research Design

Diane Davis and Marjorie Leppo

> Young scholars, although not exclusively, are trying to invent new forms of research that they believe are better suited for studying the educational worlds they care about.
>
> —Eisner (cited in Munroe-Chandler 2005)

When conducting your action research, a dilemma often faced is deciding whether the research will be characterized by a quantitative or qualitative approach. Often, however, research questions can be best answered by combing these approaches in a Mixed Methods research design. The Mixed Methods research design capitalizes on the uniqueness of quantitative and qualitative differences, while also capitalizing on the synergy between the two approaches.

Chapter Objectives

By the time you finish reading and thinking about this chapter you will be able to do the following:

- Define and describe the characteristics of the Mixed Methods research design
- Discuss the characteristics of quantitative and qualitative research methods and how each supports the other

- Discuss the value of using the Mixed Methods research design when conducting action research
- Describe and give examples of the data-gathering techniques that can be employed using qualitative and quantitative data

Why Use a Mixed Methods Approach?

A renewed and increased interest in classroom-based research continues to emerge in schools and universities across the country, as "data-driven" teaching strategies are gaining support. This impetus is largely due to teachers who now view their classrooms as rich venues for using data to improve and affirm the curriculum, their teaching practices, and the impact on students.

As you have seen in your own classrooms and read about in previous chapters, there are a variety of data available to you as a teacher researcher, both quantitative (e.g., attendance, referrals, standardized test scores) and qualitative (e.g., anecdotal records, rating scales, video/audio tapes) that can provide important information for school/student improvement.

The selection of the Mixed Methods research design in conducting action research can serve to strengthen your overall study and plans for continued action based on your results.

Simply put, when quantitative *and* qualitative techniques are mixed in a single study, you are using a Mixed Methods research design. The Mixed Methods research design provides an opportunity for the researcher to interconnect quantitative and qualitative data sources. In many situations, the researcher may even convert qualitative data into quantitative data for additional analysis. For example, qualitative data are often presented in narrative form, where the researcher summarizes the results obtained. Some qualitative data may be represented through percentages and visually placed in tables or charts. By using your skills of analysis, synthesis, and evaluation, you can extrapolate your qualitative data into a valid form of quantitative data and use it as a supportive addition to your research findings. Qualitative data also gives you an opportunity to explore and see clearly the beliefs and attitudes of those involved in the school. This may help explain why particular data results are appearing.

Additionally, quantitative or "hard data" alone often tells an incomplete or partial story. When enhanced with qualitative or "soft data," an explanation might emerge, because background information or reasons why the hard data turned out as it did can be explained.

Throughout this chapter you will be guided through the various characteristics and philosophical frameworks for the use of Mixed Methods research design. Examples are provided that illustrate the use of Mixed Methods research within the school environment.

As you conduct your own action research, you can use a Mixed Methods research design as an appropriate approach to achieve the following:

1. Probe deeper into places to answer questions pertaining to what, where, how, and why students achieve or fall short
2. Seek a greater understanding of the student's and the teacher's role in the learning process
3. Facilitate cooperative problem solving among teachers
4. Encourage reflection individually or as a part of a team approach, including students, teachers, counselors, administrators, and other stakeholders engaged in the teaching-learning community (Gay, Mills, and Airasian 2006)
5. View research efforts as an ongoing process and the potential for even broader applications of their endeavors
6. View the potential of action research as a significant part of professional development and school improvement
7. Engage in the ongoing structured practice of reflection, which is critical to improve one's teaching and learning environment

Mixed Methods versus Either-Or

The Mixed Methods research design often outweigh the benefits of using an either-or (quantitative or qualitative) approach when conducting action research because

- Each approach can generate types of information the other cannot.
- Only when the qualitative and quantitative perspectives are used together can a complete picture of the phenomenon be formed.
- Quantitative studies are good at establishing "what," while qualitative studies help us understand "how" a program succeeds or fails.
- Both quantitative and qualitative methods involve strengths and weaknesses; however, they are not mutually exclusive strategies for research. By looking at research with a broader view, the research question becomes the primary ingredient in determining the methodology of choice. (Patton, as cited in Munroe-Chandler 2005)

Philosophical Difference: Quantitative and Qualitative Data

It is important to understand the underlying philosophical differences between quantitative and qualitative data. A brief review of the characteristics of quantitative and qualitative research methods described below (adapted from Glickman, Gordon, and Ross-Gordon 2006) highlights the differences in intent for each philosophical position.

1. What is the nature of reality and knowledge?

Quantitative Response
It is based on the assumption that there is a single, external reality. Knowledge consists of objective measurements of phenomena that are part of that reality. Complex phenomena can be broken down into simple variables that can be studied independently. Eventually, the study of component variables leads to an overall understanding of a phenomenon, which in turn can lead to predictions and control of the phenomenon.

Qualitative Response
It is based on the assumption that the world consists of multiple realities that are constructed by individuals or groups. Knowledge comes with understanding of an individual's or group's assumptions, relationships, intentions, actions, perceptions, and feelings within a given context while maintaining an unbiased perspective. A phenomenon can only be studied holistically. Since each phenomenon is unique, prediction and control of future phenomena are unlikely.

2. What are the goals of research?

Quantitative Response
Its goal is to identify relationships between variables, explain causes, predict and control phenomena, and develop knowledge that is generalizable to other contexts. Quantitative research determines if a relationship exists and to what degree between two or more quantifiable variables and sometimes uses these relationships to make predictions.

Qualitative Response
Its purpose is to describe phenomena from the perspective of participants, discover multiple realities, and develop a holistic understanding of individual and group phenomena within particular contexts.

3. What is the researcher's role?

Quantitative Response
The researcher assumes the role of the detached observer. The purpose of detachment is to avoid bias. This detachment extends to the researcher's relationship with the study or the subjects.

Qualitative Response
The researcher and the study will interact and affect each other. The qualitative researcher intentionally becomes deeply involved with the phenomenon being studied. The researcher attempts to develop empathy, trust, and even friendship with the study's participants. The researcher documents interactions with the study and its participants, and critically examines his or her effects on the research and results.

4. What is the importance of context in research?

Quantitative Response
A phenomenon can be studied independently of its context. The researcher attempts to develop context-free generalizations.

Qualitative Response
A phenomenon is greatly influenced by its particular context. The whole is greater than the sum of its parts.

5. What is the relationship of cause and effect?

Quantitative Response
The response assumes that every effect can be explained by a preceding cause or combination of causes. It attempts to identify cause-effect relationships.

Qualitative Response
The response assumes that variables that are part of a phenomenon are mutually and simultaneously affecting each other. Thus it is impossible to separate causes from effect.

6. How should research studies be designed?

Quantitative Response
A blueprint for study is developed. A hypothesis is stated. A research design is selected. Instruments and subjects are selected. Data are collected. Data are analyzed using statistics to reduce bias or error, control for extraneous variables, support or refute the hypothesis, and indicate to what extent results can be generalized.

Qualitative Response
The researcher searches for evidence and understanding of processes and relations. The research sample can be small and purposeful. Data methods include observations, interviews, surveys containing open-ended questions,

searching for concepts, hypotheses, and models. Data collection and analysis are cyclical and interactive, seeking in-depth knowledge of particular phenomena.

Forms of Data

As you begin to determine the type of data you want to collect, it is important to recognize that data come in different forms. Data typically are categorized within one of four categories of variables. Nominal/categorical variables classify persons or objects into two or more categories. These types of data can be qualitative or quantitative, depending on how the researcher reports the results (numerical or narrative). Examples of these variables are gender, employment, type of school, and ethnicity.

Such data, while in categories, many times can be represented by numbers that allow the researcher to present results in graph form. Examples are the data presented on state assessment web pages, where student categories are graphically represented. Ordinal variables classify persons or objects and rank them. Examples include class rankings, socioeconomic status, one person weighs more than another, and so on. Interval variables have equal intervals, but an interval scale does not have a true zero point. Examples of these variables are tests such as achievement and aptitude tests. Ratio variables are the highest level of measurement and have a true zero point. Physical measures are an example of a ratio variable.

Tips for Working with Quantitative Data

Quantitative data are typically numerical data. After it is obtained, it can be converted into graphs or charts to analyze and interpret the results. Typical quantitative student data include formative, summative, and standardized student test scores; student demographics such as gender, ethnic background, age, and geographic location; and student profiles such as gifted, special needs, and reduced-lunch recipients.

When you are planning your research investigation, consider the following techniques to collecting quantitative data. Different types of surveys are designed to elicit responses to questions (Likert scale, typically) that focus on a specific topic that allows the researcher to gather "opinion" data from key school personnel (teachers, administrators, staff, students, and parents). Scores are represented by a number scale, which can be represented by percentages or other descriptive techniques. Tracking data represent performance over a given length of time. Examples of tracking data are derived from various populations that relate to the research investigation (students, parents, teachers, administrators, and other school personnel). A third technique is an experimental study that typically includes a control and experimental group.

Tips for Working with Qualitative Data

While qualitative data are often perceived as "soft data" (and generally not subject to statistical analysis), they provide a rich understanding of the subject's experiences that otherwise might not be achieved through an analysis of the numbers (Munroe-Chandler 2005). Qualitative data is grounded in daily interactions that take place within the school setting (MacLean and Mohr 1999). It helps you gain a more in-depth understanding of the subjective experience of the subject that might otherwise have been overlooked. It permits broader and more in-depth probing when investigating subjects and their situations (Eisner, cited in Munroe-Chandler 2005). Thus a fuller description of how the subject "perceives and interprets his/her world" is provided (Munroe-Chandler 2005). Qualitative data does not attempt to make generalizations to a larger population but is "tools for reflection and new insights" (Bain, cited in Munroe-Chandler 2005).

Figure 4.1 provides a quick reference on some of the types of data sources available to conduct qualitative research.

Useful Examples of Mixed Methods Research Design

The following six action research examples were conducted by novice action researchers during an internship experience.

Example 1 (Action Research Conducted by Rosemary Dove and Laura Jones)

The elementary school implemented a schoolwide behavior program focusing on social skills, Stop and Think. A "behavior-oriented" action research study was implemented with eight students identified as needing additional behavioral support. Students were placed into two groups that met twice a week for fifteen-minute lessons on respect.

Research Question
How does a small group intervention of social skills education make a difference in the behavior of students identified as "frequent flyers," as measured by time-out data, office discipline referral, and peer mediations?

Quantitative Data
  Student profiles
  Peer mediation

Figure 4.1. Approaches for collecting qualitative data.

Technique	Sources for data collection
Intern's daily plan book	Annotated lesson plans—what was covered, what worked or not and why
Intern's record book	Students' attendance, grades, health concerns
Intern's anecdotal records	Students' behavior, parental conferences, copy of notes written on students' work
Students' daily work folder	Compilation of students' written work, art work, quizzes, tests, projects
Students' records	Record of students' changes in behavior, including work and social behavior individually and in groups, in the classroom, cafeteria, gymnasium, playground, halls
Rating scales	Students' assessment of their own performance
Rating checklist	Checklist to denote behavioral and performance changes over time using one-word indicators (Johnson 2005)
Reflective writing journal	Evaluation of personal performance, overall students' performance, daily, weekly, monthly, and year end performance, developing a research focus (Sagor 2005)
Reflective interviews with colleagues	Planned discussion of a specific topic under investigation (Sagor 2005)
Field notes	Quick notes and detailed notes of insights and daily events (Johnson 2005)
Minutes of meetings	Provide a primary source of data that can support research question
Press clippings	Provide evidence that documents a particular subject under investigation
Video and audiotapes	Recording of verbal and nonverbal student behavior and performance (Johnson 2005)
Surveys	Open/closed questions involving students, colleagues, administrators, on assorted topics (Johnson 2005)
Attitude and rating scales	Assessment of students' attitudes via students' responses to various statements (Johnson 2005)
Product and performance rating scale	Assessment form to assess projects and creative work based on descriptive terms (Johnson 2005)
Case studies	Individual or groups of students (Johnson 2005)
Artifacts	Date and time stamp, correspondence from administrators, health professionals, materials regarding schoolwide events, copies of bulletin board materials, newspaper accounts of school events
Portfolios	Used by students to submit performance-based documentation to demonstrate successful mastery of presented material (photographs, writings, drawings, homework)
Sociogram	Social context within classroom based on student interviews (Hubbard and Power 2003)

Naturalistic and simulation observation	Students behavior occurring naturally and behavior of individuals and team role playing (Gay and Airasian 2003)
Mapping	Level of students' knowledge through the use of various mapping techniques, mapping demographic characteristics and the effect on level of academic performance
Focus groups	Discuss specific questions in a small group to gain insight into a particular issue
Phenomenological interview	Interviewee viewed as the expert; questions target learning more about the subject's experiences versus supporting the researcher's hypothesis (Dale, as cited in Munroe-Chandler 2005)

Time-out data
Office discipline referrals

Qualitative Data
Teacher surveys
Administrative and staff interviews
Observations before study, during study, and after study

Quantitative Results
All students came from difficult personal circumstances. Five of the six students were at academic risk based on reading assessments. Three of the six students were in class with a teacher with no formal training in the Stop and Think program.

Qualitative Results
Staff interviews revealed different options on the length of time the Stop and Think program had been implemented. There was no consensus about the secondary behavior intervention for frequent flyers.

Recommendations/Implications
Researchers determined that the small-group sessions did provide good results. However, all teachers need to receive formal training. Also, new students to the school need to have an orientation.

Using the Mixed Methods approach in this action research project allowed the teacher-candidates to reveal that while the results of their study were positive, the program could bring about better results if those who were delivering the program had received better staff development prior to implementation. In this example, the qualitative data supported the quantitative data results.

Example 2 (Action Research Conducted by Lindsey Plourde and Sarah Baxter)

The teacher-candidates worked collaboratively with the faculty members within the mathematics department at a high school that was searching for ways to improve algebra test scores in order to successfully meet annual yearly progress (AYP).

Research Question

Which algebra support program (1-credit algebra or algebra with assistance [AWA] class) provides a higher level of academic performance as indicated by unit test scores?

Quantitative Data
    Unit summary
    Assessment scores
    Question analysis

Qualitative Data
    Teacher and student surveys

Quantitative Results

When comparing the data from the unit tests, the researcher found that the 1-credit algebra class consistently scored higher than the AWA class.

Qualitative Results

Student surveys indicated that in both groups, students found math boring, and they were confused by having two math classes a day. Teachers of the AWA felt frustrated because of lack of planning time together.

Recommendations/Implications

The researchers made several suggestions to the members of the high school community. The principal, after reviewing the research, informed the researchers that several of the suggestions were going to be implemented.

Example 3 (Action Research Conducted by Connie Furlan and Jessica Vitrano)

The teacher-candidates assisted in data collection on a school project to implement a mentoring program for ninth graders who were identified as at-risk, for being unprepared to meet high school requirements.

Research Question
How can a mentoring program assist at-risk ninth-grade minority students in making a successful transition to high school?

Quantitative Data
    Interval grades
    Attendance records
    Suspension records
    Student data records on the Maryland State Report Card

Qualitative Data
    Surveys completed by mentors
    Interviews completed by students
    Classroom observations

Results
The overall results indicated that the mentoring program was beneficial and had a positive effect on the students involved in the program. Students who were mentored missed fewer days of school. GPA went up from first to second semester. Students would recommend the program to other students. Students had different reasons why they were identified as at-risk. Those who received mentoring were less likely to be suspended.

Recommendations/Implications
It was recommended that the program continue and that the middle school needs to provide additional information to make the program even stronger. The mentoring is ongoing and the high school plans to enhance the program.

Example 4 (Action Research Conducted by Dan McGonigal and Kristina Lowery)
The teacher-candidates wanted to determine if there was improved achievement by students after teachers were exposed to a professional development activity.

Research Question
What is the relationship between a schoolwide intervention and the improvement of achievement scores among fourth- and fifth-grade minority males?

Quantitative Data
  Demographic information
  Maryland State Assessment (MSA) scores
  Classroom scores on reading and math
  Attendance
  Student mobility
  Interventions
  Behavior issues

Qualitative Data
  Questionnaire
  Discussion with intervention specialists
  Student surveys

Results
While data were correlated on several demographic elements such as gender and MSA scores, the intervention did not correlate with the needs specifically enough to moderate achievement changes among the fourth- and fifth-grade minority males.

Recommendations/Implications:
Created a faculty professional development focus group: Faculty were asked to read, study and discuss key elements of the book *Hear Our Cry: Boys in Crisis.* Interventions need to be specifically aligned to the child's needs to be effective.

Example 5 (Action Research Conducted by Elizabeth Bana and Karolyn Burley)
The teacher-candidates wanted to determine if there was improved achievement by students who were a part of the Achievement Via Individual Determination (AVID) program.

Research Question
To what degree is the implementation of the AVID program successful in meeting the needs of students within high school settings?

Quantitative Data
  Demographics
  Learning disabilities
  Free and reduced meals

Graduation rate
College enrollment

Qualitative Data
Survey of ninth- and twelfth-grade AVID students
Observations

Results
Results of the ninth-grade qualitative data indicated an improvement in grades and more interest in college. They benefited from the social aspects of the AVID program. The twelfth-grade data demonstrated more of a focus on doing well in classes and preparing themselves for life after high school.

Recommendations/Implications
The results indicated that the AVID program is successful at the high school at its current level. It was recommended that a longitudinal study be conducted to determine the long-term impact of the AVID program after high school graduation.

Example 6 (Action Research Conducted by Katie Haynes, Kristan May, Stephanie Mester, and Monica Wilson)
The teacher-candidates wanted to determine if there was improved student behavior after the implementation of a behavior management plan.

Research Question
To what extent is the newly implemented behavior management plan (BMP) successful in improving student behavior?

Quantitative Data
Climate survey (completed by students, faculty, and staff)
Office referrals from the past two years
Bus referrals from the past two years

Qualitative Data
Interviews with teachers and parents

Results
The newly implemented behavior management plan is working at the school. However, poor behavior on the bus and among males is still higher than desired.

Recommendations/Implications

The researchers recommended that the BMP be implemented with more emphasis on the buses. They suggested professional development for faculty—reading *"Hear Our Cry: Boys in Crisis,"* by Paul D. Slocumb. Enhance communication with parents about the BMP.

Triangulating Data within a Mixed Methods Research Design

One of the major advantages of using Mixed Methods research design is the concept of triangulation. By definition, triangulation is a process for probing and securing an "in-depth understanding of the phenomenon" under investigation (Denzin and Lincoln, as cited in Munroe-Chandler 2005). Triangulation gives you, the researcher, an opportunity to use multiple data sources to collaborate your findings and ask the question: *Does one data source support another?*

An example of the use of the triangulation approach is provided in the study above, in which the researchers asked the question: *How can a mentoring program assist at-risk ninth-grade minority students in making a successful transition to high school?* They used interval grades, attendance records, suspension records, and student data records on the Maryland State Report Card as their quantitative sources and used surveys completed by mentors, interviews completed by students, and classroom observations to gather qualitative information. This type of data gathering gives action research substance and also provides validity to the results. If you only use one type of data source, you may be tempted to draw an inaccurate conclusion or make inappropriate recommendations.

Conclusion

The Mixed Methods research design provides a practical approach to conducting action research. This approach allows you to gain a more precise answer to research questions within the classroom and school environment. Using the Mixed Methods research design allows you to put to use the multitudinous forms of quantitative and qualitative data readily available in your teaching and learning environment.

Questions for Review and Reflection

1. Define each of the following terms and give an example of each: *quantitative data, qualitative data,* and *triangulation.*

2. Describe at least four differences between quantitative and qualitative research methods.
3. How do quantitative and qualitative research methods support each other?
4. Define what it means to use a Mixed Methods research approach.
5. Explain the practical application of the use of the Mixed Methods research design approach within a school setting.

References

Eisner, e. w. (1997). The new frontier in qualitative research methodology. *Qualitative Inquiry*, 3, 259–27.

Gay, L. R. & Airasian. (2003). *Educational research competencies for analysis and applications* (7th ed.). New Jersey: Pearson Education.

Gay, L. R., Mills, G. E.,& Airasian, P. (2006). Educational research competencies for analysis and applications (8th ed.). New Jersey: Pearson Education.

Glickman, C. D., S. P. Gordon, & J. M. Ross-Gordon. (2006) *SuperVision and instructional leadership: A developmental approach* (7th ed). Boston, MA: Allyn and Bacon

Hubbard, R. S. & Power, B. (2003). *The art of classroom inquiry: A handbook for teacher-researchers*. Revised edition. New Hampshire: Heinemann.

Johnson, A/P. (2005). *A short guide to action research* (2nd ed.). Boston: Pearson Education.

MacLean, M. S. & Mohr, M. M. (1999). *Teacher-researchers at work*. California: National Writing Project Corporation.

Munroe-Chandler, K. J. (2005) A discussion on qualitative research in physical activity. *Athletic Insight The Online Journal of Sport Psychology*. Retrieved October 20, 2008, from http://www.athleticinsight.com/vol71Iss1/qualitativeresearch.htm.

Sagor, R. (2005). The action research guidebook A four step process for educators and school teams. Thousand Oaks, Student Development: Items 9–16, 26–29. California: Corwin Press.

CHAPTER FIVE

Action Research Video Studies for Improving Classroom Teaching-Learning Performances

Linda A. Catelli

This chapter is devoted to assisting teachers, teacher candidates, their supervisors, and teacher educators in conducting video-based action research studies to change and improve classroom teaching and learning. The information provided will also be useful to in-service teachers who are actively engaged in inquiry groups, learning communities, professional development, or master's degree programs.

The use of videotaped analysis, reflection, and assessment can be instrumental to improving student learning and furthering the teacher's development as an effective and reflective practitioner. Three powerful video strategies—*microteaching*, *self-study*, and *interaction analysis*—coupled with examples of observational tools and an *action research perspective* are offered as ways to accomplish this purpose. Also, helpful hints to supervisors, mentors, teachers, and teacher educators are interspersed throughout the chapter along with relevant research and resources for readers to draw upon.

The main focus, however, is on you and your interest in improving classroom performances through action research video studies and projects. This information can be used in a variety of settings (e.g., professional development schools) and for a range of subject areas and grade levels (e.g., science, music, and grades pre-K through 12). The action research process (issue identification, data collection, action planning, plan activation, and outcome assessment), the study of teaching, videography, and a *working framework* for changing classroom teaching-learning performances toward more desirable outcomes are all highlighted in this chapter.

Chapter Objectives

By the time you finish reading and thinking about this chapter you will be able to do the following:

- Explain the *action research perspective* that is promoted throughout the chapter for your video-based study or project. Briefly describe how descriptive observational systems and video were developed, and how they are currently used in the field of education.
- List ways in which you might use descriptive observational systems for your video-based action research study.
- Describe each of the three video strategies you might use for your project: (a) microteaching, (b) self-study, and (c) interaction analysis.
- Apply the action research process to your own video-based research study.

An Instructional Set for Readers

Before we begin, it might be best to supply you with an instructional set. In the following three sections of this chapter, you will take a journey that will provide you with some history, research, and the specific tools you will need to conduct a video-based action research study or project. The goal is to help you change and improve teaching and learning in your classroom.

The journey will begin with "The Study of Teaching: A Historical Overview," about the pioneers who have used video as either a research or feedback tool to improve teaching and learning. You might already be asking yourself, "Why read about the history of the study of teaching?" Well, the answer is that this section provides you with a specific *action research perspective* and vantage point from which to base, anchor, and conduct your video study.

Most of the information in the chapter is derived from a research perspective that attempts to link the study of classroom teaching to classroom learning—i.e., teaching-learning performances. The perspective embraces action research for its action qualities and process, and it encompasses research on teaching effectiveness for its expressed connection to student learning. Thus it has become for me, as well as for others, an *action research perspective*. Proponents of this perspective seek to link teaching to learning in their studies. Their interests lie in understanding the relationship between teaching and learning, and the effects of teaching on learning. Thus, the action research perspective adopted here greatly influences how you frame your action research questions (step 1, issue identification), how you design and implement your action video study (steps 2–4, data collection, action planning, plan activation), and how you interpret the findings (step 5, outcome assessment).

Situated within a historical overview of the study of teaching are three powerful strategies for conducting your video-based action research project—*microteaching, self-study,* and *interaction analysis.* These three video strategies are highlighted and explained. The procedures for implementing each are outlined for you (action planning and plan activation). You should emerge from the first section with a solid understanding of the action research perspective for your study, how the perspective emerged, and an understanding of the three video strategies. Also, you should be able to identify the ways in which descriptive observational systems are used to collect and analyze video data.

In the second section, titled "On the Road to Becoming Effective with Video," you will get a glimpse of summarized relevant research findings as guides from teacher effectiveness research and what is sometimes called process (teacher actions)-product (student outcomes) studies. Such questions as "What do effective teachers do in the classroom?" and "What is good teaching?" are answered by illuminating recent research findings.

You should emerge from this part of the chapter being able to identify (a) the four performance domains that can be observed using video recordings, and (b) two to three research-based guides for effective teaching that fall within your interest. This section is not meant to provide you with narrow prescriptions but rather to offer you general guides of action to investigate, which as you learned in chapter 1, help you identify issues for study.

This second section concludes with examples of topics, questions, and areas you might focus on for your study or project. The general focus areas and questions are derived directly from the action research perspective. They are offered to spark your interest and assist you in refining an area and topic to investigate, along with reviewing some research on teaching effectiveness. If you have a different research question to base your study on, that is fine. This section, however, is still valuable for you to peruse for current research. Before you read the third and final major section of the chapter, make sure that you have (a) sketched out a focus area and topic that interest you, and (b) drafted a series of research questions that relatesto both your topic and focus area in step 1 of the action research process, issue identification. Also, you should have in mind one of the three video strategies presented.

The last major section, titled "Mirrors for Analysis, Reflection, and Assessment," provides you with specific examples of descriptive observational systems and sources of rubrics for you to (a) collect and analyze your video performance data (step 2 of the action research process), (b) reflect on your performance and that of your students relative to the goals and video strategies you may have selected (steps 3 and 4 of the process), and (c) assess how well you and your students have engaged in desirable actions relative to the learning outcomes and student gains that have accrued (step 5 of the action research process). The use of the observational tools in video studies that connect teaching to learning is promoted here. Also, making sure that you recognize that there is an array of observational tools for you to use is an outcome of the section.

Finally, in the last part of the section titled "Putting It Together," I place the three video strategies (microteaching, self-study, and interaction analysis) in a *working framework* that you may use to conduct a video-based project. The use of any one of the three strategies makes for a powerful action research design to help you systematically improve teaching-learning performances in your classroom.

As you have learned throughout this book, linking best practices or pedagogical actions to standards-based outcomes and student achievement is certainly popular today. You should consider both as possible video projects. Also, you should consider using newer technologies and commercial software packages that now make it possible to conduct more sophisticated video studies than in the past. By the end of the final section, you should be in a good position to conduct a video-based action research study or project.

The Study of Teaching: A Historical Overview

Why study teaching? Teaching has long been the focus of study by educators, researchers, and philosophers in education. Their inquiry originated from their desire to understand, define, and improve teaching. Why understand teaching? Why improve it? The significance of such an endeavor lies in the fact that this society values education and sees education as a means for bettering itself and the world.

As Philip Jackson has explained in his two seminal works, *The Way Teaching Is* and *Life in Classrooms*, teaching is basically a moral activity that has social significance. Educators and researchers, whether they are interested in developing new knowledge, helping students construct their knowledge, or facilitating a person's self-fulfillment, are ultimately striving to improve society and life in the society.

Viewed as a series of intentional acts, teaching in the classroom is one of the main vehicles through which a formal education happens. If we improve the process of classroom teaching-learning then the ultimate goal set forth by educators and researchers to improve life in the society has a better chance of being realized.

Given the social significance of teaching, it is easy to understand why it has long been the target of study and why so many researchers and action researchers are constantly searching for ways to solve classroom problems to improve teaching and learning.

Early Research on the Study of Teaching and the Action Research Perspective

Prior to 1950, research on the study of teaching was concerned primarily with investigating the relationship of teacher characteristics and teaching methods with effectiveness in classroom teaching. Studies that attempted to either compare instructional methods for their effects on student achievement or identify significant teacher personality traits (e.g., orderliness) for their effects on student achievement virtually flooded the literature at the time.

The search for "good" teacher traits or "good" and "better" methods was viewed by many researchers as a means of providing the knowledge necessary to improve teaching and thus enhance learning. For the most part, the search for answers was unsuccessful. One reason why researchers were unsuccessful was their inability to adequately capture classroom teaching in a natural setting. Audio and video recording technology had not yet arrived on the scene!

Regardless of all the research efforts prior to 1950, it was the consensus of most reviewers that the findings from these early investigations yielded very little useful knowledge about teaching (Gage 1963, 1966; Jackson 1966; Anderson 1971). Also, it was thought that too many researchers at the time were trying to arrive at final judgments about teaching effectiveness without first understanding the phenomenon itself.

Recognizing the fruitlessness of their attempts to study and improve teaching, many researchers shifted the focus of their inquiry and adopted a new and different approach to studying and improving teaching. Their inquiry was now redirected to "analyzing" the teaching process itself and providing accurate "descriptions" of what actually occurs during classroom events and teacher-student interactions.

In an effort to improve upon the past, leading researchers elaborated on this new approach by proposing a research plan or paradigm for those interested in conducting what is sometimes referred to as "classroom research." This type of research plan came to be known as the descriptive-correlational-experimental loop or paradigm (see Rosenshine and Furst 1973). Researchers and action researchers who implemented the first part of the plan conducted what was called descriptive-analytic observational action studies. Those researchers who continued on to the second and third parts of the loop conducted correlational, process-product, and experimental studies. Thus, the work of describing teaching and studying the effects of teaching on learning (or teaching effectiveness) became a *research perspective*.

Past and present education researchers and action researchers who adhere to this perspective strive to link or connect classroom teaching to learning in their research plans. They want to understand the relationship between the two in order to improve education. Also, they want to investigate the effects of teaching actions on learning, and the impact that organizational, managerial, and social-climate factors have on student performance. Observation via the use of videography is crucial to the action research process. Thus, this *action research perspective* forms a particular vantage point for your video-based action research study. It influences to a large extent how you will frame your action research issues and questions, how you will design and plan your study, and how you will collect and interpret data (as described in chapter 1, steps 1–5 of the action research process).

The Development and Use of Descriptive Observational Systems

In adopting the new paradigm in the 1950s and 1960s, leading researchers of the time such as Ned Flanders (1960, 1970), B. O. Smith (1962, 1963a, 1963b), Arno Bellack (1963, 1966), as well as many others, began to implement the stages of the "loop" by developing and using observational tools, or what we call descriptive observational systems. They used the systems to capture teacher or student, or teacher and student interactive behaviors in classroom settings. Their main intent was to describe and understand teaching and its relationship to learning in a natural setting (see Dunkin and Biddle 1974).

It was during this period of time (1950s to the late 1970s) that hundreds of these descriptive observational systems were developed. The systems included sets of categories that captured different aspects of classroom life and events such as classroom management and discipline (e.g., Kounin 1970), verbal and nonverbal communication (e.g., Galloway 1968), and student behavior (e.g., Spaulding 1963, 1970). The systems were used as observational tools to record frequencies and the duration of teacher-student behaviors, and to collect data about teaching and learning and the relationship between the two.

Those researchers who went on to conduct correlational and process-product studies of the research paradigm/loop often incorporated descriptive observational systems in their investigations so as to provide precise data about teaching and learning. Other researchers, as well as teacher educators, began to develop and use the systems not only as research tools to study and improve teaching but also as feedback tools to provide information to the teachers who were being observed.

As feedback tools, these systems served to help pre- and in-service teachers gain greater insight into their classroom actions and interactions. It provided them with a way of reflecting on their interactive behaviors with students and analyzing their instructional actions in relation to their stated learning goals for students. Thus, the use of descriptive observational systems became prevalent not only in research but also in teacher education. Finally, what emerged from this early period were the following purposes or uses for descriptive observational systems in education:

- To describe and analyze current classroom practice
- To investigate relationships between classroom actions/activities and student achievement
- To document changes and the effects of teacher-student actions over time
- To prepare teachers to use instructional strategies and provide them with feedback so as to improve their teaching performance to effect learning positively
- To monitor and assess the teacher's instructional actions in accord with the goals of a new educational program and the desired student performances

This list provides you and your teacher educator with the varied ways in which the systems are also used today, and the ways you might use descriptive observational systems for your own video project. Which one might interest you?

The Emergence of Video to Study Teaching-Learning and the Three Video Strategies

Concurrent with the development and use of the observational systems (1960s to the 1980s) was the emergence and use of video technology in research and in teacher education. Because video equipment had become less expensive and more transportable in the sixties, many researchers and teacher educators began to use video to study to improve teaching.

Pioneering researchers such as Bruce Joyce, Arno Bellack, William G. Anderson, and their doctoral students at Teachers College, Columbia University were using audio and video recordings to develop observational systems and to collect data as part of their research and action studies.

Teacher educators were using video and descriptive observational systems with preservice students to help them develop specific teaching skills, or to provide them with feedback about their performances of instructional methods (e.g., guided discovery). Or they were using video along with the observational systems to help preservice students reflect on their classroom interactions with students. In addition, principals were using video along with the observational systems as instructional devices to help in-service teachers acquire new pedagogical practices that accompanied newer programs in reading, mathematics, and social studies. And they were using video and the available systems as supervisory devices to assist teachers in improving their teaching to increase learning.

In the research arena, William G. Anderson and his doctoral students at Teachers College conducted one of the first large-scale video projects and data bank, which involved taping more than eighty classes in randomly selected regions of New York, New Jersey, and Connecticut (Anderson and Barrette 1978). The data and findings from the video studies of the project were useful for establishing a video library and for understanding what actually occurred in classes from both the teacher's and students' perspective.

Developing your own personal video library and data bank of findings is a neat project for you to consider. It is an excellent way for you to chart your development and that of your students over time. Segments and clips from your digital video library can be analyzed and inserted into electronic portfolios or papers as mouse-clickable multimedia links and citations. The segments might be used as observable evidence of improved teacher and student performances. Also, it might be interesting to compare or model your video classroom performances with the performance data from the Third International Mathematics and Science Study (TIMSS), another large-scale video project (Stigler and Hiebert 1999). Other large-scale research video projects you might want to draw upon for ideas are Project STAR—Student/Teacher Achievement Ratio (Mosteller, Light, and Sachs 1996), and Lesson Study (Lewis and Baker 2010).

During the seventies, eighties, and well into the nineties, researchers, principals, and teacher educators were increasingly using video and descriptive observational systems in their work.[1] During this period of time, three important video strategies emerged from the worlds of teacher preparation and education research: microteaching, self-study, and interaction analysis. The three strategies were and are, still to this day, effective in studying and improving classroom teaching-learning performances. They are explained below for your consideration for your video-based action research project or study. The one you might select will become an integral part of the design and plan for your study, representing steps 2, 3, and 4 of the action research process.

Microteaching, Self-Study, and
Interaction Analysis: Tools for Action Research

Microteaching

Microteaching, used extensively in teacher education by Bruce Joyce (1972) and his then associates at Teachers College (TC), is a strategy that enables an individual to practice a teaching skill (e.g., leading a discussion) or an entire instructional model (e.g., group investigation) in a series of teach and reteach cycles of videotaped minilessons. The lessons are taught to a small group of peers or students. Between lessons, the individual watches his or her videotaped performance with or without a supervisor.

The purpose of viewing the tape is to have the individual analyze his or her performance to determine whether or not he or she was successful in performing the teaching skill or method of instruction and to determine the effects the performance had on student learning (Brent, Wheatley, and Thompson 1996; Allen and Ryan 1969). At TC, descriptive systems were used by Joyce and his doctoral students to code the taped performances of lessons taught by interns to small groups of pupils enrolled in TC's laboratory school, the Agnes Russell Elementary School. Narratives and critiques of the taped performances were subsequently made, and evidence of student learning was submitted as part of the final analysis and evaluation of the interns' lessons.

The idea in using videotapes was to reduce the complexity of the teaching-learning situation so that preservice teachers or interns could focus on developing the pedagogical skills associated with a model of teaching. Also, the purpose was to analyze and research the model's effects over time on student learning. In this context, microteaching proved to be an extremely powerful strategy for improving the preservice teacher's performance of pedagogical skills associated with each of Joyce's models of teaching and improving student learning. Also, it proved to be a powerful strategy for school improvement. As a member of the lab school at the time, I can attest to its effectiveness.

You should consider using microteaching for your video-based action research project. The strategy can be used in your field setting, professional development school, or methods courses. It is an excellent video strategy for (a) acquiring new pedagogical skills/methods, (b) getting feedback and improving classroom performances, and (c) monitoring student achievement in a more manageable environment (Joyce and Showers 1988, 2002). Also it is a strategy that fits well with the action research process—i.e., the steps and cycles that you learned about in chapter 1. I have used it consistently in my work in teacher education and in the action research studies I have conducted in schools (see Catelli 1990, 1995; Catelli, Padovano, and Costello 2000).

Finally, upon its arrival, as Sherin (2008) has commented, microteaching quickly "became the standard for teacher education programs nationwide" (3). It remains as effective today as it was when it was first introduced.

Self-Study

In addition to his large-scale video project and data bank, W. G. Anderson (1971, 1980) created a process for preservice and in-service teachers to systematically analyze and improve their teaching along with evaluating student achievement. This systematic, self-analytic process, similar to the action research process, basically involves twelve steps:

1. Observing what happens during a class via video or peer observations
2. Compiling a record of those observations using descriptive observational systems or other recording methods
3. Analyzing, interpreting, and evaluating the record
4. Making decisions about the needed changes for future classes based on the findings
5. Monitoring the changes toward the desired teacher actions or best practices
6. Evaluating student improvement and achievement
7. Developing in writing your own personal beliefs and concept of teaching-learning
8. Translating the written concept into specific pedagogical actions and student actions
9. Examining the record (findings) for any discrepancies between your concept and your actual record of teaching performances—that is, seeing if your records are consistent with your concept and if you are doing what you believe in philosophically
10. Making any necessary changes to bring your teaching performances into closer alignment with your concept, beliefs, research, and your understanding of how students learn
11. Designing criteria for evaluating the match between your lesson plans and actual classroom occurrences
12. Designing criteria for evaluating teaching-learning performances and student achievement

Thus, as seen in the last two steps, the final evaluation and assessments are not based on outside criteria but rather on criteria that are developed by the teacher. The criteria are drawn from the teacher's own written beliefs and concept of teaching-learning.

This systematic, self-analytic process as developed by Anderson included clinical tasks that proved to be an excellent strategy for (1) ensuring consistency in beliefs and actions, (2) matching lesson plans with actual classroom actions, and (3) improving teaching to effect student learning. I label it as the *self-study* strategy and offer it to you for conducting your video-based action research project. The strategy may also be used jointly by you and your mentor for developing your professional concept of teaching-learning.

Interaction Analysis

Interaction analysis is the third powerful video strategy for improving classroom teaching-learning performances. It emerged during the earlier periods of the study of teaching-learning. The strategy makes use of video and descriptive observational systems. The systems often include sets of categories that represent specific student and teacher interactions (e.g., teacher asks a higher-order question, student responds and initiates a comment). The systems are used by observers to code a videotaped lesson or a series of lessons.

In interaction analysis, preservice or in-service teachers are trained to use a system to analyze their actions and interactions in relation to a specific learning goal. For example, if the teacher's overall goal is to have students become creative writers, then the performance of certain teacher-student interactions that are compatible with that goal (e.g., accepting and extending student ideas) is important to achieving the goal. Or if a teacher is interested in knowing how much time he or she spends presenting information as compared to the amount of time he or she has students practice the desired skill, the system is used to provide that type of descriptive information. Teachers often make changes based on the information they obtained from coding their videotaped lesson. And they often used the resulting codes from the video to evaluate the effects of their specific actions on student performances of the desired learning outcomes.

The most popular of all the observational systems that were used to capture classroom interactions was the one developed by Ned Flanders in 1960. It was called the Flanders Interaction Analysis Categories (FIAC) (Flanders 1960, 1970; also see Amidon and Hough 1967).

Consider interaction analysis as a third powerful video strategy to study teaching and the effects of your teaching on learning. It is a strategy that lets you obtain descriptive data from which to base your decisions, and to make your own evaluations while collecting evidence to make judgments about student engagement, learning, and achievement. Also, evidence and findings can be viewable segments of taped performances over time, along with artifacts of student work, test scores, and so on, and teacher work samples.

Triangulating data sets is certainly possible as well as using a Mixed Methods approach (see chapter 4). The Flanders system has been successfully adapted and used with preservice students and teachers in many action research video studies that were important components of two school-college partnerships and one PDS partnership (see Catelli 1995, 2002; Catelli and Carlino 2001; Catelli, Carlino, and Longley 2002; Catelli, Carlino, Cantillo, et al. 2007 for information and action research within the partnerships). An adapted version of the Flanders system is seen in table 1 in appendix A of this chapter.

So, now that you have a little history and three relevant video strategies, and you know how descriptive observational systems are used in education, it is now time for you to know what we have learned from past research on the study of teaching-learning. Acquiring this information will bring you closer to selecting and refining a topic for your study. Keep in mind the action research perspective, the five-step process, and the three video strategies.

On the Road to Becoming Effective with Video

Over the past four and a half decades, research findings from the study of teaching effectiveness have provided us with empirical knowledge about teaching and learning (Floden 2001; Richardson 2001). Such research has led us to understand that student learning gains are strongly related to the quality of the teacher (Fergerson 1998; Goldhaber 2002; Goldhaber, Perry, and Anthony 2004; Hanushek 1992; Sanders and Rivers 1996; and Wright, Horn, and Sanders 1997). Further, we have learned from more recent research that "teaching effectiveness" in classrooms is

- context specific (Campbell, Kyriakides, Muijs, and Robinson 2004; Muijs and Reynolds 2005)
- associated with the teacher's ability to perform specific instructional actions that are linked to learning goals
- ultimately, dependent on the teacher's knowledge of subject matter and his or her knowledge of how students learn and develop (Darling-Hammond and Baratz-Snowden 2005; Darling-Hammond and Bransford 2005; Bransford, Brown, and Cocking 2000; Donovan, Bransford, and Pellegrino 1999)

With the recognition that it is the quality of the teacher and his or her effectiveness in the classroom that makes the difference in student learning, it then becomes important for you to know what specific teacher actions are associated with teaching effectiveness. Thus, this part of the chapter answers the questions *What do effective teachers do in the classroom?* and *What is good or effective teaching?* The information in table 2 in appendix B of this chapter is certainly not exhaustive. I have selected from summaries of research those instructional actions and best practices that are performed in the classroom and are easier to observe, analyze, and assess via videography.

Table 2 in appendix B is not meant to provide you with narrow pre-scriptions for your video study but rather to supply you with some general research-based guides of action on effective teaching to investigate. They are offered as a way of assisting you in (1) changing and monitoring your interactions with students toward more desirable instructional performances, (2) linking your teaching actions with student performances and learning outcomes, and (3) solving classroom problems or issues. I have drawn the guides of action from primarily four sources:

L. Darling-Hammond and J. Baratz-Snowden, *A Good Teacher in Every Classroom*
P. Chance, *The Teacher's Craft: The Ten Essential Skills of Effective Teaching*
P. D. Tucker and J. H. Stronge, *Linking Teacher Evaluation and Student Learning*
P. Kauchak and D. Eggen, *Learning and Teaching: Research-Based Methods*

Finally, the information seen in table 2 in appendix B is organized around the questions identified above and four major performance domains of teaching-learning: (1) the social climate and atmosphere of the classroom, (2) classroom management and the physical environment, (3) classroom instruction, and (4) student engagement. Take a moment to read through the listing in table 1, and then select one or two performance domains along with two researched-based guides of action that either interest you or that relate to your issue (step 1 in the action research process).

Focus Areas and Sample Questions for Your Video Study or Project

At this point in the journey you should have a solid understanding of (a) the action research perspective—linking teaching to learning, (b) the varied uses of video and descriptive observational systems in education, and (c) the three video strategies for improving teaching-learning. Also, you should have selected one or two performance domains and two research-based guides for effective teaching that interest you or that relate to your issue.

Having accomplished the above, it will now be important for you to select a specific focus area for your video-based project. The focus areas presented below are examples. They were formulated based on the action research perspective and effective teaching guides of action seen in table 2 in appendix B. You should read through the list carefully to determine if any match with your previous selections. Record the ones that closely align with your interest and selections. Or you may create a focus area to meet your own particular needs.

Possible Focus Areas (FA#)

1. Monitoring changes in teacher and student interactions over time and then measuring the effects on student performance and learning (FA1)
2. Measuring the learning effects of your performance of specific (a) lessons or units of instruction, (b) methods of instruction, (c) models of teaching-learning, or (d) theories of teaching and learning (e.g., multiple intelligences) (FA2)
3. Monitoring your lesson plans and classroom actions over time for consistency with your professional concept and beliefs about teaching-learning, and then measuring the effects on student performance (FA3)
4. Developing and performing specific teaching skills (e.g., asking higher-order questions) and instructional strategies (e.g., leading discussions) to effect (a) increases in student engagement and on-task behavior and/or (b) increases in the level and quality of student thinking during discussions (FA4)
5. Acquiring and performing new programs, methods, or models of teaching-learning (e.g., jigsaw, group investigation, etc.) to improve student learning gains and outcomes (FA5)
6. Linking your teaching actions to professional standards and providing evidence of student learning or achievement (FA6)
7. Developing a video library and data bank of findings for charting your progress and that of your students in a particular subject area or grade level (FA7)
8. Developing a video library and data bank of findings for a case study of a student in any one or all of the performance domains (FA8)
9. Describing and assessing current classroom performances with reference to effective teaching actions or teacher-student interactions and their effects on student performance of the learning outcomes (FA9)

Having selected (a) one to two performance domains (e.g., classroom instruction and student engagement), (b) two effective teaching guides that you are interested in as general topics for your study (e.g., instructional questions and students' engagement [table 1]), and (c) a possible focus area (e.g., FA9 —describing and assessing current classroom performances with reference to effective teaching action, etc.), the next step is to create a set of research questions that will guide your video study.

To assist you, I have identified as an illustration a set of questions that an action researcher might formulate for a video study based on the examples seen in the parentheses above. So let us say, for example, that you are interested in classroom instruction and student engagement as the performance domains, and more specifically you are interested in the instructional questions you ask of your students. You are particularly interested in knowing the effects of your questions on student engagement and learning performances. Further, you want to find out what you currently do; assess what you do; and perhaps change what you do for purposes of linking the types of questions you ask to measures of effectiveness on student learning performances and student engagement. Such thinking may result in the set of research questions identified in sample A.

Sample Topic and a Set of Questions: A. *Asking Instructional Questions*

Of the total time I spend in a lesson or unit for which questions play a major role in achieving the objective(s), how much of the instructional time do I devote to asking students questions? What types of questions do I ask (e.g., higher-order, lower-order, or probing)? What is the ratio of the high to low questions? Is there a pattern in terms of the sequence (e.g., low, low, high; high, high, low, high)? What specific level of thinking do the questions provoke (e.g., memory, comprehension, analysis, evaluation, synthesis)? Which levels are important to achieving the objectives and learning outcomes of the unit? What levels are revealed in the students' responses? Do I ask questions to check for understanding? Do I extend students' thinking and ask them to explain their answers or thoughts? What levels and types of thinking are taking place during the students' small-group discussions? Do my questioning strategies differ for students assessed at lower levels of ability? Do my strategies differ for students at higher levels of ability? How would I assess or rate my performance? How would I assess the students' performances? Based on an analysis of the video data and the answers to these questions, what do I want to do differently in subsequent lessons? What changes will I make and for what reasons? Over a series of taped lessons, what changes have taken place? What comparisons can I make? What are the effects of the changes on student performances and on the learning outcomes? What improvements can be readily seen? What additional evidence supports the improvements that have taken place?

To answer the questions for sample topic A, you would need to videotape a series of lessons and use one or more descriptive observational systems and rubrics as video tools. You would need to use the tools to collect, analyze, monitor, and assess your video performances, as well as document evidence of change. In addition, it would be important for you to collect and analyze artifacts of student work, test scores, and video clips of student performances along with conducting student surveys and interviews. Of course, for your video studies, you may need to secure permission from parents, teachers, and perhaps from the Institutional Review Board (IRB).

Mirrors for Analysis, Reflection, and Assessment

This last section is arranged for you in three parts. Continue to do what is requested and you will be in a good position to conduct your video project. The first part of the section provides you with examples of descriptive observational systems and suggested rubrics you might use to (a) collect, analyze, and document your video performance data; (b) reflect on your performance and that of your students; (c) assess how well you and your students have engaged in research-based actions; and (d) link teaching to learning.

The descriptive systems serve as mirrors for viewing classroom performances. They will help you see your classroom actions and events in a somewhat more objective, systematic, and descriptive manner. They are not used as tools to evaluate your instructional interactions, but rather as tools to descriptively document them. How well you or your students performed will be assessed in two ways: first, by you, in terms of the degree to which you have achieved your stated goals along with the extent to which your students have performed the desired learning outcomes; and second, by the use of rubrics, rating scales, and other appropriate teacher-student performance criteria.

The second part of the section provides you with sources of rubrics and assessment systems. And finally in the third part, I offer you a working framework to design, plan, and conduct your video-based action research study. The framework pulls together the chapter's information in order to help you change and improve teaching-learning performances in your classroom. I conclude our journey and the section by enumerating the major benefits of using video.

Using Descriptive Observational Category Systems for Your Video Study

Descriptive observational category systems can focus on teacher or student actions, or they can focus on the interactions between teachers and students. The exemplar system (seen in table 1 in appendix A of this chapter) is a version of the Flanders system created for a series of video studies conducted recently within a PDS. The system is entitled "An Adaptation of the Flanders Observational Category System of Interaction Analysis" (see Catelli and Carlino 2001; Catelli, Carlino, Cantillo, et al. 2007; Catelli, MacLauren, et al. 2008; and Catelli, Frampton, et al. 2009 for its adaptation and use). The system focuses on teacher-student interactions.

The Flanders system (1960, 1970) is still one of the most widely used in research. The original system classified teacher-student interactions into ten categories. The adapted system classifies teacher and student instructional interactions into twenty-five categories, each of which is represented by a number. Table 1 in appendix B includes descriptions of the categories and their definitions. An observer/coder learns the system before coding a taped performance. Having prepared a recording form prior to the observation, as shown in figure 5.1, the coder records a tally mark every five seconds next to the category number that best represents the action observed (the original system had coders recording every three seconds).

For example, if a teacher praises a student, the coder records a tally mark next to 2a. If two actions occur during the five-second interval (e.g., teacher presents information to the class and asks a lower-order question), then both actions are recorded for the interval (e.g., 5a and 4a). At the completion of the observational period, the tally marks are totaled for each category and a grand total is computed for the frequency column (f). A percentage is then computed for each category indicating the amount of time or the percent of time the student or teacher engaged in a particular classroom action.

We can determine from the analysis (a) how time was spent by the teacher during a lesson, (b) which instructional actions the teacher engaged in and for how long, (c) how much time the students were engaged, and (d) how much time the teacher devoted to management and discipline versus instruction. If we want to know about the sequence of teacher actions (e.g., asking questions, giving feedback, etc.), the coder uses a coding sheet as shown in figure 5.2 to record the category numbers in succession. Patterns of instructional actions and interactions are revealed with this method of coding. The

Figure 5.1.   Sample recording form.

Category Number	Tally Marks	f	%
1			
2a	/		
2b	/////		
3			

Grand Total =

Figure 5.2. Sample coding sheet.

1.	5	4.	5	7.	
2.	5	5.	4a	8.	
3.	5	6.		9.	

adapted Flanders system (Catelli and Carlino 2001) makes use of a recording form and/or coding sheets to record classroom actions and interactions.

You should know that there are many descriptive observational systems available to capture the various dimensions of classroom life. Some spotlight management and discipline such as the one developed originally by Kounin (1970) (for an updated version, see Good and Brophy 2004). Others analyze the social climate/atmosphere of the classroom (e.g., Spaulding 1963, 1970; CLASS by Pianta, Paro, and Hamre 2008). Still others highlight specific pedagogical interactions as in Brophy-Good's dyadic system (2008), the Adapted Laubach system for student actions (see Catelli 1995; Catelli, Padovano, and Costello 2000), and the Fishman system for categorizing teacher feedback (Anderson and Barrette 1978).

There are even descriptive-analytic category systems to analyze "conferencing behaviors" of principals with teachers, and supervisors with their student teachers (see Kindsvatter and Wilen 1982; Glickman, Gordon, and Ross-Gordon 2004). Thomas Good and Jere Brophy in *Looking in Classrooms* have identified a number of observational systems and other techniques such as checklists, rating scales, and anecdotal records to capture classroom life. I highly recommend the book as an additional resource. There are many observational systems available for you to choose from for your video project. Which one(s) you choose to use will depend on your topic and research question(s). Also, you may create your own observational tools or adapt an existing one to suit your purposes. In addition, you may alter the coding forms, time intervals, and procedures for coding.

Finally, descriptive observational systems provide an account of what you and your students do during lessons. They help you connect teaching to learning. As feedback tools, they also help you monitor changes over time toward desired actions and effective instructional performances. As research tools, they assist you in comparing findings and data from earlier lessons with data collected from later lessons. Also, they help you measure the effects of your teaching. Charting your progress and that of your students is an important use of the observational video tools. The resulting data and segments of taped performances should be used to provide visible evidence of student learning and achievement.

Using Rubrics and Assessment Criteria for Your Video Study
The information derived from descriptive observational systems tells you
what classroom interactions were performed but not *how well* they were performed. Rubrics and performance assessment criteria can be used to provide
that information. Educational Testing Service's *PATHWISE* is a registered
program that provides excellent performance criteria and scoring rubrics
for evaluating nineteen teaching areas (ETS 1995). The teaching areas are
arranged in four domains, which are similar to the performance domains
mentioned previously.

As is the case with most teaching rubrics, instructional actions are assessed by observers using performance criteria and a rating scale of 1.0 (low)
to 3.5/4.0 (high). Detailed descriptions and the criteria for the instructional
actions are outlined in the *PATHWISE Orientation Guide* (ETS 1995,
31–41). You can secure information and perhaps an updated version of the
PATHWISE guide by contacting ETS at www.ets.org/pathwise. PATHWISE
has been used extensively to evaluate novice teachers and student teachers
in many different settings. The domains are based on Danielson's *Enhancing
Professional Practice: A Framework for Teaching* (2007). If you are unable to
secure the guide from the website, go to Danielson's book for the rubrics.

Another set of rubrics for assessing classroom performances comes from
the state of California. California's Performance Assessment for California
Teachers—PACT (2007) was designed by a group of educators to measure
the competence of teacher candidates in relation to the Teacher Performance Expectation (TPE). It is used to meet the California Commission on
Teacher Credentialing (CCTC) requirements for teacher certification. More
specifically, the rubrics are currently used to assess the candidate's ability to
perform when placed in an actual teaching situation. Videotaped segments
of the candidate's performance are submitted for review. The PACT rubrics
can be accessed at www.pacttpa.org/rubrics/.

The National Board for Professional Teaching Standards requires appli-
cants to submit videotapes capturing segments of lessons that illustrate the
quality of their teaching. The segments along with other artifacts are evaluated using rubrics with a rating scale of 1.0 (low) to 4.0 (high). The rubrics
may be found in the National Board's *Middle Childhood/Generalist Standards
Scoring Guide* (1998). To obtain an updated scoring guide, go to www.nbpts
.org/ and type "scoring guide generalist middle childhood" in the search box.
Then click submit, and you can download a recent guide in PDF. Select the
parts that deal with video.

Rubrics and assessments have been adapted and used successfully from all
three sources mentioned above in action research studies with partnering

teachers, preservice teachers, and graduate students at Dowling College.[2] Findings from the studies were used to change instructional performances and improve aspects of a teacher education program that was clinically based at the Belmont Elementary Professional Development School in New York. Other resources you may want to draw upon for additional rubrics, instruments, and observational protocols are the following:

- *Looking Inside the Classroom: A Study of K-12 Mathematics and Science Education in the U.S.* (2003) at Horizon Research: www.horizon-research.com (click "instruments")
- National Comprehensive Center for Teacher Quality (2008a, 2008b)

There are numerous student and teacher rubrics available on the Internet for you to use. All of the descriptive systems and rubrics mentioned can be used separately or in conjunction with computer software. The computer software applications will help you code, analyze, and organize the digitized videotaped performances more efficiently. Two companies that offer software licenses at reasonable prices are Studiocode and Noldus. We are soon approaching the day when coding a tape by hand will be a thing of the past.[3]

A Working Framework for Putting It Together

For the final part of the journey, a simple working framework is presented, as shown in figure 5.3. The working framework is designed to assist you in putting all the information together. The ideas put forth in the framework are based on the action research perspective promoted throughout this chapter and the action research process steps 1–5, described in chapter 1. The ideas are springboards for thought and are by no means inclusive of all the possibilities for your video study or project.

The working framework has four features: goal and focus area; questions; video strategy; and sample tools. The first feature or column refers to the overall goal and purpose for conducting your video-based action research study. The goal statement is followed by a bracketed number representing the specific focus area from the previous section your goal is most compatible with (FA#). The goals identified in the framework are samples. Based on the goal statement you have selected, you will then want to formulate a series of research questions. I have left that column blank for you to fill in the information.

The research questions you formulate are specific to your investigation and your previous choices of performance domain(s), research-based guides of action, and general topic (step 1, issue identification). Of course, you

Figure 5.3. A working framework.

Goal and focus area	Questions	Video strategy	Sample tools
To acquire and use a method or model of teaching-learning to improve student learning outcomes [FA5]		Microteaching	Flanders system Rubrics (T & S)
To develop and perform specific teaching skills/strategies to effect increases in student engagement and learning [FA4]		Microteaching	Flanders system Laubach system Fishman system Rubrics (T & S)
To monitor changes in student and teacher interaction over time and then measure the effects on student learning and achievement [FA1]		Interaction analysis	Flanders system Laubach system Rubrics (T & S)
To measure the learning effects of specific lessons and units, or to monitor performance changes and improvements over time [FA2]		Interaction analysis	Flanders system Laubach system Rubrics (T & S)
To develop and implement a professional concept of teaching-learning and measure its effects on students [FA3]		Self-study	Flanders system Laubach system Fishman system Rubrics (T & S)
To develop a video library and data bank of findings for charting your progress and that of your students [FA7]		Self-study	Flanders system Laubach system Rubrics (T & S)

may refer to the sample set of questions I presented previously as examples. Under the heading "video strategy," the strategy that best accomplishes the goal is identified (steps 2 and 3, data collection and action planning). For the procedures that are used to implement each strategy, I suggest you refer to an earlier section of the chapter where the strategies were explained in detail (step 4, plan activation).

The last column of the framework is titled "Sample tools." In this column, I have listed descriptive observational systems and the types of rubrics (T & S—teacher and student) that can be used to collect, analyze, monitor, and assess video performance data (steps 2/5). The resulting data can be used as evidence of change, improvement, or evidence that the desired learning outcomes have been achieved (step 5, outcome assessment). Other artifacts of your work (e.g., lesson plans, reflective narratives) or student work (journals, projects, tests) may also be used to provide evidence, along with video clips.

Final Comment: The Benefits of Using Video

The benefits of using digitized video are numerous. The seven benefits that quickly come to mind are these:

1. It provides a permanent record that you can return to, to conduct subsequent analyses.
2. It captures both the teacher's and students' perspective.
3. It can be edited in segments so that you focus on a particular aspect of classroom actions. For example, if you are investigating your questioning strategies within a unit, you may want to extract from a series of lessons all those instances that involve questioning.
4. Video allows for a more authentic assessment of teaching.
5. It provides visible evidence of student learning and achievement.
6. It provides visible records of changes and improvements over time.
7. It documents evidence of the effects of teaching and teaching effectiveness.

Certainly, the use of video in professional portfolios and in hypermedia and multimedia teacher education programs affords exciting new opportunities for educators. As a video action researcher, you have an exhilarating time ahead of you. Without a doubt, in this new era of education reform and renewal, the use of videography and action research to improve classroom teaching-learning performances takes center stage!

Questions for Review and Reflection

1. What is the action research perspective that is promoted throughout the chapter for your video-based study or project? How did it emerge and how were descriptive observational systems and video used in the field of education? How might you use the descriptive observational systems to conduct your action research project?
2. What are the three video strategies presented for your consideration? Explain the video strategy that you might use for your video-based action research study.
3. Which performance domain(s), action guide(s), general topic(s), and focus area(s) interest you the most?

4. Using the working framework and the examples presented in the chapter, (a) formulate and refine a set of research questions that relates to both your chosen goal-focus area(s) and topic(s); (b) identify the video strategy and sample observation tools and rubrics for your study; and (c) use the tools, rubrics, and other artifacts to collect and analyze the data for answering your research questions and linking teaching to student learning or achievement.

References

Allen, D., and K. Ryan. 1969. *Microteaching*. Reading, MA: Addison-Wesley.

Amindon, E. J., and J. B. Hough, eds. 1967. *Interaction analysis: Theory, research, and application*. Reading, MA: Addison-Wesley.

Anderson, W. G. 1971. Descriptive-analytic research on teaching. *Quest* 15:1–8.

———. 1980. *Analysis of teaching physical education*. St. Louis, MO: C. V. Mosby.

Anderson, W. G., and G. T. Barrette. 1978. *What's going on in gym: Descriptive studies of physical education classes*. Monograph. Newton, CT: Motor Skills: Theory into Practice.

Bellack, A. A., and J. Davitz. 1963. *The language of the classroom: Meanings communicated in high school teaching*. New York: Institute of Psychological Research, Teachers College, Columbia University.

Bellack, A. A., R. T. Hyman, F. L. Smith Jr., and H. M. Kliebard. 1966. *The language of the classroom*. Final report, USOE Cooperative Research Project, No. 2023. New York: Teachers College, Columbia University.

Bransford, J., A. Brown, and R. Cocking, eds. 2000. *How people learn: Brain, mind, experience, and school*. Washington, DC: National Academy Press.

Brent, R., E. Wheatley, and W. S. Thompson. 1996. Videotaped microteaching: Bridging the gap from the university to the classroom. *The Teacher Educator* 31 (3): 238–47.

Brophy, J. E. 2008. *Using video in teacher education*. Bingley, UK: Emerald.

Campell, J., L. Kyriakides, D. Muijs, and W. Robinson. 2004. *Assessing teacher effectiveness*. New York: RoutledgeFalmer.

Catelli, L. A. 1990. Teaching the teaching process: Reflections and strategies at an urban college. *Teaching Education* 3 (1): 89–101.

———. 1995. Action research and collaborative inquiry in a school-university partnership. *Action in Teacher Education* 16 (4): 25–38.

———. 2000. The adapted Laubach system of student action. Unpublished document. Dowling College.

———. 2002. Project SCOPE I &and II: Holistic school-college/university partnership projects for instituting change and improvement in K–18 education. In *Commitment to excellence: Transforming teaching and teacher education in inner city and urban settings*, ed. L. A. Catelli and A. Diver-Stamnes, 73–116. Cresskill, NJ: Hampton Press.

Catelli, L. A., and J. Carlino. 2001. Collaborative action research to assess student learning and effect change. *Academic Exchange Quarterly* 5 (1): 105–12.

Catelli, L. A., J. Carlino, G. Cantillo, T. Starke, and K. Greene-Batt. 2007. Teacher candidate classroom performances in a professional development school setting: Parts I-III of an action research video project. Unpublished document. Dowling College.

Catelli, L. A., J. Carlino, and C. Longeley. 2002. Action research video studies: Student teacher classroom performances in a school-college partnership project. Paper presented at the fifty-fourth annual meeting of the American Association of Colleges for Teacher Education, New York, February.

Catelli, L. A., K. Frampton, D. Nienburg, J. Pati, M. Salle, N. Weidler, A. Weissback, K. Zummo, L. DelPrete, and C. Stupiello. 2009. Teacher candidate classroom teaching performances in a professional development school setting: Part V of an action research video project. Unpublished document. Dowling College.

Catelli, L. A., N. MacLauren, M. deRozieres, A. Labushor, M. Sampson, L. Schock, A. Eaton, M. Duffy, K. Dean, and T. LaFauci. 2008. Teacher candidate classroom teaching performances in a professional development school setting: Part IV of an action research video project. Unpublished document. Dowling College.

Catelli, L. A., K. Padovano, and J. Costello. 2000. Action research in the context of a school partnership: Its values, problems, and benefits. *Educational Action Research* 8 (2): 225–42.

Chance, P. 2008. *The teacher's craft: The ten essential skills of effective teaching.* Lake Grove, IL: Waveland Press.

Danielson, C. 1996. *Enhancing professional practice: A framework for teaching.* Alexandria, VA: Association of Supervision and Curriculum Development.

———. 2007. *Enhancing professional practice: A framework for teaching.* 2nd ed. Alexandria, VA: Association of Supervision and Curriculum Development.

Darling-Hammond, L., and J. Baratz-Snowden. 2005. *A good teacher in every classroom.* San Francisco: Jossey-Bass.

Darling-Hammond, L., and J. Bransford. 2005. *Preparing teachers for a changing world.* San Francisco: Jossey-Bass.

Donovan, M. S., J. D. Bransford, and J. W. Pellegrino. 1999. *How people learn: Bridging research and practice.* Washington, DC: National Academic Press.

Dunkin, M. J., and B. Biddle. 1974. *The study of teaching.* New York: Holt, Rinehart and Winston.

Educational Testing Service (ETS). 1995. *PATHWISE: Orientation guide.* Princeton, NJ: Author.

Fergerson, R. 1998. Teachers' perceptions and expectations and the black-white test score gap. In *The black-white test score gap*, ed. C. Jencks and M. Phillips, 273–317. Washington, DC: Brookings Institution Press.

Flanders, N. A. 1960. *Interaction analysis in the classroom: A manual for observers.* Ann Arbor: University of Michigan.

———. 1970. *Analyzing teacher behavior.* Reading, MA: Addison-Wesley.

Floden, R. E. 2001. Research on effects of teaching: A continuing model for research on teaching. In *Handbook of research on teaching*, 4th ed., ed. V. Richardson, 3–16. Washington, DC: American Educational Research Association.

Gage, N. L. 1963. *Handbook of research on teaching*. Chicago: American Educational Research Association/Rand McNally.

———. 1966. Research on cognitive aspects of teaching. In *The way teaching is (Report of the Seminar on Teaching)*, 29–44. Washington, DC: Association for Supervision and Curriculum Development and the Center for the Study of Instruction of the National Education Association.

Galloway, C. M. 1968. Nonverbal communication. *Theory into practice* 7:172–75.

Glickman, C. D., S. P. Gordon, and J. M. Ross-Gordon. 2004. *Supervision and instructional leadership*. Boston: Pearson.

Goldhaber, D. 2002. The mystery of good teaching: Surveying the evidence on student achievement and teachers' characteristics. *Education Next* 2 (1): 50–55.

Goldhaber, D., D. Perry, and E. Anthony. 2004. NBPTS certification: Who applies and what factors are associated with success? *Educational Evaluation and Policy Analysis* 26 (4): 259–80.

Good, T. L., and J. E. Brophy. 2004/2008. *Looking in classrooms*. Boston: Pearson.

Hanushek, E. A. 1992. The trade-off between child quantity and quality. *Journal of Political Economy* 100 (1): 84–117.

Jackson, P. W. 1966. The way teaching is. In *The way teaching is (Report of the Seminar on Teaching)*. Washington, DC: Association for Supervision and Curriculum Development and the Center for the Study of Instruction of the National Education Association.

———. 1974. *Life in classrooms*. New York: Holt, Rinehart and Winston.

———. 1990. *Life in classrooms*. (Second printing). New York: Teachers College Press.

Joyce, B., and B. Showers. 1988. *Student achievement through staff development*. New York: Longman.

———. 2002. *Student achievement through staff development*. 3rd ed. Alexandria, VA: Association for Supervision and Curriculum Development.

Joyce, B., and M. Weil. 1972. *Models of teaching*. Upper Saddle River, NJ: Prentice Hall.

Joyce, B., and M. Weil, with E. Calhoun. 2004/2009. *Models of teaching*. Boston: Pearson.

Kauchak , P., and D. Eggen. 2007. *Learning and teaching: Research-based methods*. Boston: Allyn & Bacon.

Kindsvatter, R., and W. Wilen. 1982. A systematic approach to improving conferencing skills. In *Perspectives for reform in teacher education*, ed. E. Grimsley and R. Bruce, 4–22. Englewood Cliffs, NJ: Prentice Hall.

Kounin, J. S. 1970. *Discipline and group management in classrooms*. New York: Holt.

Lewis, C., and E. Baker. 2010. Action research through the lens of lesson study. In *Action research for teacher candidates: Using classroom data to enhance instruction*, ed. R. Pelton. Lanham, MD: Rowman & Littlefield.

Mosteller, F., R. J. Light, and J. A. Sachs. 1996. Sustained inquiry in education: Lessons from skill grouping and class size. *Harvard Educational Review* 66:797–842.

Muijs, D., and D. Reynolds. 2005. *Effective teaching: Evidence and practice*. Thousand Oaks, CA: Sage Publications.

National Board for Professional Teaching Standards (NBPTS). (1998). *Middle childhood/generalist scoring guide*. San Antonio, TX: Author.

National Comprehensive Center for Teacher Quality. 2008a. *Approaches to evaluating teacher effectiveness: A research synthesis.* Washington, DC: Author.

———. 2008b. *Key issue: Using performance-based assessment to identify and support high-quality teachers.* Washington, DC: Author.

Performance Assessment for California Teachers (PACT). 2007. Rubrics: PACT teacher performance assessment. www.pacttpa.org/rubrics/ (accessed April 7, 2008).

Pianta, R. C., K. M. Paro, and B. K. Hamre. 2008. *Classroom assessment scoring system: Mannual K–3.* Baltimore: Paul H. Brookes Publishing.

Richardson, V. 2001. *Handbook of research on teaching.* 4th ed. Washington, DC: American Educational Research Association.

Rosaen, C. L., M. Lundeberg, M. Cooper, A. Fritzen, and M. Terpstra. 2008. Noticing noticing: How does investigation of video records change how teachers reflect on their experiences? *Journal of Teacher Education* 59 (4): 347–60.

Rosenshine, B., and N. Furst. 1973. The use of direct observation to study teaching. In *Second handbook of research on teaching.*, ed. R. M. Travers. Chicago: Rand McNally.

Sanders, W. L., and J. C. Rivers. 1996. *Cumulative and residual effects of teachers on future student academic achievement.* Knoxville: University of Tennessee Value-Added Research and Assessment Center.

Sherin Gamoran, M. G. 2008. New perspectives on the role of video in teacher education. In *Using video in teacher education,* ed. J. Brophy, 1–27. Bingley, UK: Emerald.

Simon, S., and E. G. Boyer. 1970. *Mirrors for behavior: An anthology of observation instruments.* Philadelphia: Research for Better Schools.

Smith, B. O. 1962. Conceptual frameworks for analysis of classroom social interaction. *Journal of Experimental Education* 30 (4): 325–26.

———. 1963a. A conceptual analysis of instructional behavior. *Journal of Teacher Education* 14:294–98.

———. 1963b. Toward a theory of teaching. In *Theory and research in teaching,* ed. A. A. Bellack. New York: Teachers College Press.

Smith, B. O., and M. O. Meux. 1963. *A study of the logic of teaching.* Urbana: University of Illinois Press.

Spaulding, R. L. 1963. Achievement creativity and self-concept correlated of teacher-pupil transactions in elementary schools. Cooperative Research Project No. 1352, College of Education, University of Illinois.

———. 1970. Categories for a coping analysis schedule for educational settings. In *Mirrors for behavior: An anthology of observational instruments,* ed. A. Simon and E. G. Boyer. 2 vols. Philadelphia: Research for Better Schools.

Stigler, J. W., and J. Hiebert. 1999. *The teaching gap: Best ideas from the world's teachers for improving education in the classroom.* New York: Free Press.

Tucker, P. D., and J. H. Stronge. 2005. *Linking teacher evaluation and student learning.* Alexandria, VA: Association for Supervision and Curriculum Development.

Wang, J., and K. Hartley. 2003. Video technology as a support for teacher education reform. *Journal of Technology and Teacher Education* 11 (1): 105–38.

Waxman, H. C., R. C. Tharp, and R. Hilberg. 2004. *Observational research in U.S. classrooms*. New York: Cambridge University Press.

Wright, S. P., S. P. Horn, and W. L. Sanders. 1997. Teacher and classroom context effects on student achievement: Implications for teacher evaluation. *Journal of Personnel Evaluation in Education* 11 (1): 57–67.

Notes

1. For an in-depth explanation of how video was used in teacher education, see the excellent chapter written by Miriam Gamoran Sherin titled "New Perspectives on the Role of Video in Teacher Education," in Jere Brophy's *Using Video in Teacher Education* (2008). Also see Simon and Boyer, *Mirrors for Behavior* (1970), for an anthology of earlier descriptive observational systems.

2. Over a three-year period (2006–2009), the Dowling College–Belmont Elementary PDS Partnership personnel (e.g., teachers, teacher candidates, professor-director, etc.) conducted a series of three action research video studies that were aimed at instituting change and improvement in the classroom teaching performances of teacher candidates. The studies were part of a larger project entitled Action Research Video Project: Parts I–V. For more information about each of the three studies, please see Catelli, Carlino, Cantillo, et al. (2007); Catelli, MacLauren, et al. (2008); and Catelli, Frampton, et al. (2009).

3. For information about research on using video as a reflective tool and the use of video technology for teacher education reform, see Rosaen et al. (2008) and Wang and Hartley (2003).

Appendix A: Observational Tools and Recording Forms
Table 1   An adaptation of the Flanders Observational Category System of Interaction Analysis

1. ACCEPTS FEELINGS/SETS CLIMATE AND CREATES A SENSE OF COMMUNITY: Accepts and clarifies an attitude or the feeling tone of a student in a nonthreatening manner. Feelings may be negative or positive. Predicting or recalling feelings—past, present, or future—is included. Or the teacher makes comments to affect the climate positively in order to release tension and contribute to productive communication and a positive learning environment. Humor and jokes that release tension, not at the expense of another, are included. Or the teacher facilitates participation in meaningful discussions that develop student ideas and opinions and their respectful consideration of others' points of view.

2a. PRAISES OR ENCOURAGES: Praises or encourages student action or behavior for the purpose of providing an attitudinal-motivational set. Nodding head or saying "yes," "OK," "um hum," or "go on" and/or making comments to affect the student's psychological state positively— e.g. "try your best," "I know you can do it," "you'll do better next time."

2b. GIVES CORRECTIVE FEEDBACK: Gives specific evaluative, prescriptive, descriptive, and/or explicative feedback to influence, guide, or monitor one or more student performances in learning content or a skill (mental or motor). Evaluative comments that assess or appraise the performance can be positive or negative—e.g., "good, excellent" or "no, you're doing it incorrectly." Feedback is about the performance and can occur during or after the student has performed.

3. ACCEPTS, USES, OR EXTENDS IDEAS OF STUDENTS: Clarifies, repeats, interprets, extends, builds, develops, or elaborates on ideas suggested by a student. As a teacher brings more of his own ideas into play, shift to category 5.

4. QUESTIONS

   4a. ASKS LOWER-ORDER QUESTIONS: Asks memory-recall questions about content or procedures. Rhetorical questions are included.

   4b. ASKS HIGHER-ORDER QUESTIONS: Asks questions that encourage students to apply, explain, analyze, predict, infer, evaluate, judge, synthesize, and/or reflect. Questions that focus, clarify, and require students to elaborate or imagine are included.

   4c. ASKS PROBING QUESTIONS

   4d. PROMPTING OR CUEING

   5. LECTURES OR PRESENTS INFORMATION: Gives or explains facts, ideas, concepts, principles, and opinions about content to

   5a. The whole group

   5b. A small group within the large group

   5c. An individual (seat work or up at the teacher's desk)

   5d. Articulates the goal, objective, rubric, standard, or expectation for the lesson

   5e. Reads a story or reads a word problem

6a. GIVES DIRECTIONS—MANAGERIAL/ORGANIZATIONAL FUNCTIONS: Gives directions, commands, or orders with which one or more students must comply. Includes the teacher administering tests, handing out materials, fixing equipment, arranging or organizing groups, and transitions.

6b. GIVES DIRECTIONS—SUBJECT MATTER (CONTENT—SKILL/CONCEPT): Gives directions and procedural information about how to do something, what to do to engage in or to complete a mental or motor task. Includes re-explaining or repeating directions.

7. ESTABLISHES OR ENFORCES CODES OF BEHAVIOR: Disciplines or makes statements intended to change student behavior from nonacceptable to acceptable patterns; criticizes; bawls someone out. Or states why the teacher is doing what he or she is doing—justifying authority.

8a. STUDENT TALK—RESPONSE: Student(s) makes a response to teacher. Teacher initiates the contact or solicits student statement in a group discussion or individually, or requests a choral response from students.

8b. STUDENT ENGAGEMENT: Participating in a task/activity or discussion groups.

9. STUDENT TALK—INITIATION: Talk by students that they initiate. Shift from 8a to 9 if student introduces own ideas.

10a. SILENCE/CONFUSION: Pauses or periods where students are waiting or confused as to what is to be done.

10b. OBSERVATION (TEACHER OBSERVING): Teacher silently observes one or more students' performances and/or circulates around the room while students are engaged in individual or group tasks/activities.

10c. WAIT TIME: The pause between questions or the pause after a student answer and a teacher interruption or interjection.

11. TEACHER ILLUSTRATES-DEMONSTRATES AND TALKS

12. TEACHER TALKS AND STUDENT ILLUSTRATES-DEMONSTRATES

13. OTHER/SPECIFY

Appendix B: Research-Based Effective Teaching Guides of Action

Table 2   What do effective teachers do in the classroom? What is good teaching?

The social climate and atmosphere of the classroom—Effective teachers:

- Create an atmosphere that is non-threatening and supportive of learning. They make more positive comments than negative comments. They comment favorably on desirable behaviors more than they comment negatively on undesirable behaviors.
- Praise and encourage students.
- Listen to students and show in explicit ways that they care about and respect students.

- Create a sense of community among students by helping them interact respectfully with one another and by facilitating students' active participation in meaningful discussions that develop their expression of ideas and opinions along with their consideration of others' points of view.

Classroom management and the physical environment—Effective teachers

- Communicate clearly expectations and rules for behavior.
- Communicate clearly role expectations during group and independent work.
- Establish and reinforce procedures for daily classroom routines and tasks.
- Maintain the flow and momentum of lessons through smooth transitions of activities.
- Engage in more than one action at the same time.

- Display student work inside the classroom and outside the door.
- Have materials easily accessible when needed and efficiently distributed.
- Observe and monitor classroom events, activities, and behaviors. They anticipate potential problems and resolve minor distractions before they become major disruptions, as well as repair and restore disruptive or disrespectful student behavior.

Classroom instruction—Effective teachers:

- Communicate the goal or objective(s) of the lesson either explicitly or implicitly. They inform students of the rubrics and criteria for performance and they connect their objectives/goals to the learning activities and assessments in a coherent and meaningful way.
- Maximize allocated time for instruction so that students have ample opportunities and amounts of time to learn. Effective teachers have much higher percentages of engaged time for students than less effective teachers. Good teaching involves using available time efficiently and effectively.
- Communicate content/subject matter clearly. They have the verbal ability to present information/ideas in a clear and compelling manner, and the verbal ability to explain concepts so that students can develop understandings. They give clear examples, analogies, and representations of the content. Clarity is the most important element in communicating the subject matter—knowledge, skills (mental or motor), values, habits, and dispositions.
- Observe, assess, and provide specific feedback to students about their performances. Giving corrective feedback is crucial, especially in skills-based lessons. Good teaching involves giving feedback to individual students directed at their particular needs and based on learning progressions. It involves assessing students (formally and informally) to reveal what students know, understand, and how they are reasoning. The acts of observing, assessing, and giving feedback are usually linked to form an instructional action.
- Observe, diagnose, and correct misunderstandings and misconceptions.
- Actively conduct practice, and pace the activities and information.
- Are flexible, responsive, and can adapt instruction to meet the demands of the situation and the diverse needs of each student.
- Build an understanding through questioning and thinking tactics.
- Cover every part of the room to monitor every activity that takes place.
- Perform high levels of instructional discourse and student-teacher interactions.
- Use a variety of instructional strategies—mastery learning, guided practice, cooperative learning—to accomplish different types of learning goals and outcomes.
- Apply hands-on learning.
- Demonstrate or model what is to be done when appropriate.
- Illustrate by pictures, videos, models, diagrams, graphs, and tables to show students the point or concept.

Student engagement and involvement—Effective teachers:

- Have all students involved in challenging, meaningful, and developmentally appropriate learning activities related to desired goals and objectives. Effective teachers have higher percentages of students on task and higher percentages of time that students are engaged than less effective teachers.
- Ask students different types of questions—e.g., higher- and lower-order; probing, etc.,—for engaging students and for having them understand concepts and develop critical thinking skills. Effective teachers ask more questions than less effective teachers.
- Encourage students to formulate and initiate questions, to discuss and elaborate on their own ideas, as well as to comment on statements made by others.

PART II

PLANNING FOR SUCCESS
IN ACTION RESEARCH

CHAPTER SIX

Learning Conversations: How Oral Inquiry Supports the Five Steps of Action Research

*Stefan Biancaniello, Stephanie Cucunato,
and Sean Biancaniello*

This chapter will explore how communication supports action research. Conversations will be examined from several perspectives: conversation purpose, conversation format, and conversation types, all as interactive communicative tools to support teaching and learning research.

This chapter will guide you in the process of using conversations as a teaching and learning methodology to support your work as an action researcher, as illustrated in figure 6.1. You will learn how conversations can establish a forum where questions, ideas, and hypotheses are shared and used to better understand what is working, how it is working, and why it is working. You will learn how conversation design, when thoughtfully constructed, can expand the potential for learning. You will experience conversations that can be used as tools to engage students in the thinking and learning process, not as just passive recipients of the teaching but as genuine partners in the human learning endeavor.

Chapter Objectives

By the time you finish reading and thinking about this chapter you will be able to do the following:

- Define action research
- Examine conversation strategies that support action research and "reflection in action"

- Explore several conversation formats and types as oral inquiry methods that underpin the reflective process of action research
- Learn techniques for designing conversations that increase the impact of action research and its results

Why Learn about Conversation Strategies?

Education is a human endeavor. We think and learn through the exchange of thoughts, ideas, and beliefs. Through this interchange, our minds grow understanding. Leonid Vygotsky defines this process in a concept called "social learning theory." In chapter 1 you learned that as an action researcher you apply this concept through the practice of reflection in action, a process that supports learning through experience. In this chapter you will learn how to apply conversation strategies and techniques to increase the impact of that reflective process. We will examine conversations as a means of communication and as a fundamental building block to human learning (Moll 1990).

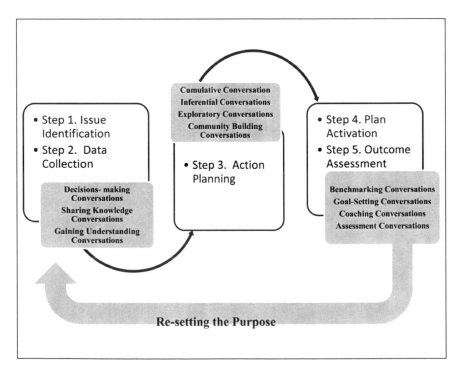

Figure 6.1.　Oral Inquiry: A Conversation Model for Action Research

Action Research: A Framework

Before we continue, it is important to provide you a framework for thinking about conversations as tools for learning and research. To accomplish this, we must establish an operational definition of action research. For this, we have selected Kemmis and McTaggart's research, which defines action research as a "deliberate process that seeks solutions through investigations of practice." To implement this definition, we will build upon the framework learned in chapter 1, the five-step action research process, which includes identifying issues, collecting data, developing action plans, implementing those plans, and finally, assessing outcomes. Conversations will be presented as a methodology for investigation and reflection.

These conversations or oral inquiry processes are not just "teacher talk"; they are a research methodology and become much more than an exchange of ideas, thoughts, discourse, or talk (Kanevsky 1993). When thoughtfully orchestrated, they create meaning and generate a purpose.

Action research is not about learning why we do certain things, but rather how we can do things better. It is about how we can change instruction to impact students. It is about turning data into knowledge and knowledge into wisdom. This transfer is accomplished through the communication of thoughts, ideas, and vision.

We can use conversations to produce a fresh new set of methods to identify important issues we face in the classroom, to capture data, analyze and synthesize information, plan and implement interventions, and assess our results. These new communicative methods provide new opportunities to learn and reflect upon your research project. The chapter will guide you through this process and help you build a mindset for reflection in action.

Checking for Understanding—Establishing Our Focus

Things to remember:

1. Vygotsky's "social learning theory" put into practice through learning conversations
2. Conversations can be used as a methodology for action research
3. The framework for action research is a deliberate process that seeks solutions through investigations of practice and is implemented in a five-step process.
4. Conversations are not just "teacher talk"; they can be a research methodology that supports action research.

5. Action research is about turning data into knowledge and knowledge into wisdom. This transfer is accomplished through the communication of thoughts, ideas, and vision.

Oral Inquiry in Action Research

The following strategies provide insight into various conversations and how they can be a methodology for supporting your action research. To increase understanding of the subtle differences that exist between the conversations, each is explained individually and set into categories where they are most effective. In reality, these conversations are fluid. It is more important to learn how the skillful use of conversations can enrich your research project, than which conversation should be used for a situation. The strategies help you differentiate your thinking about how you communicate with colleagues and students in particular situations and in seeking specific outcomes.

Establishing a Conversation Purpose to Support Action Research Step 1: Issue Identification

Learning conversations, especially those that will support action research, can and should be focused on a specific purpose. For action research to provide valuable and impacting information, your work in the research process needs to identify specific outcomes and expectations.

Careful planning of conversations can ignite thought-provoking interactions that can guide your practice. Conversations with colleagues and students provide learning opportunities to question, investigate, explore, and learn in a proactive way. They are, in fact, meaning-making activities. It is important to note here that the term *conversation* in this arena refers to much more than idle chatter, gossip, or storytelling. What we speak of here are interactions that represent the foundation of true inquiry because they are focused, directed, and orchestrated for a specific purpose with clear expectations and defined outcomes.

As you prepare for your action research project, focusing on the kinds of questions you want to explore can be enriched by also focusing on conversations that help refine your thinking and planning around those questions. These conversations, if well planned and designed, will sharpen your investigative potential. What makes a conversation work is the collaborative process that includes talking, listening, reflecting, and responding. In participating in this process, new understanding emerges, and that new understanding helps identify issues and concerns (Halliday 1993).

Depending on the outcome you seek, several kinds of conversations can be used to support your work. Each of these conversations can provide opportunities for specific lines of thinking that in turn can guide your actions.

Conversations for Decision Making

When you are attempting to decide upon a course of action or a set of parameters to guide your work, you can configure conversations that help focus on available options. Through talking, listening, questioning, and reflecting, the conversation process allows participants the opportunity to develop understanding that can then be used to support decisions.

Pointed conversations aid in practical decision-making and help socialize the thinking of participants. Sometimes they clarify issues and sometimes they expose strengths and weaknesses. But every time they produce insight. These conversations should be structured around fact finding, information gathering, and categorizing the knowledge that surfaces from verbal exchanges. Subsequently, conversations designed for decision making are built upon investigative questions that expose, elaborate, and/or define specific and focused information. As you think about your project and collaborate with mentors and colleagues, use one or more of the following question stems to focus your investigations and weigh evidence for decision-making.

These are some sample question stems:

- Does the evidence support current practice?
- Do we have enough evidence to support expanding the intervention?
- Does evidence of current practice require action?
- Which options provide the best opportunity for success?

Conversations that Exchange Knowledge

Sometimes the outcome we seek is deeper insight into the challenges we face. You may be seeking input and perspective from colleagues, mentor, or administrators. Perhaps you would like to tap the experiences of others who have addressed similar issues. In this arena, what is most important is the sharing of knowledge or the exchange of ideas with others in an attempt to refocus or refine our own thinking and planning.

With careful planning and insightful questions, we can construct opportunities for conversations that add to our collective wisdom and provide options for our actions. Well-crafted topics for conversation sequenced to unpack ideas in such a way as to stimulate the collective thinking of participants create a corridor of exchange that expands your knowledge and shares the new knowledge across roles and among colleagues. In these conversations, how you unfold the progression of topics and how you relate those topics to a common purpose become key strategies for implementation.

Notice the sequence of the question stems below. This sequence helps unpack what transpired while gathering input from others. When you seek to exchange knowledge, plan your conversation sequence well to explore ideas in a systematic way. This organization of thought and action will enhance your learning potential.

- What opportunities have presented themselves in the project?
- How have we responded to those opportunities?
- What have we learned from our thinking and action?
- What could we have done differently?

Conversation for Understanding

The challenges we face in the classrooms and with students are formidable. Examining the process of teaching and learning and developing effective interventions that directly impact learning is complicated and demanding. Conversations can and should be used to reflect, review, and reconsider ideas, thoughts, proposals, and decisions. In this capacity, conversations can help us deepen our understanding of our challenges. We can take advantage of the knowledge held by colleagues and engage in spirited conversations that sculpt the collective knowledge into understanding and then into wisdom.

Understanding is the result of making meaning in situations. Conversations that engage the diverse thinking capital of participants stimulate creativity and innovation. They increase our confidence in what we know and can do. This process grows understanding and it also helps us sort out variations, find connections, and make meaning (Wertsch 1991). So while people may enter into a conversation for a variety of purposes, all conversations result in new understandings for all participants. These new understandings can approach the trivial or may be nearer to epiphanies. It is through conversations that knowledge is exchanged and new understanding grows.

Conversations can really help focus your thinking. When you are seeking to make sense of what is happening in your action research project, question stems like the samples that follow can be used to engage your mentor and colleagues in stretching your thinking and helping you question your assumptions; both can be important for increasing your understanding of your project and its potential.

- What is the story told by the evidence?

- What if any assumptions have been validated or challenged?
- How has new learning impacted thinking and planning?
- Why did we get the results we did?

Checking for Understanding—Conversation Purposes That Support Action Research Step 1: Issue Identification

Things to remember:

1. Careful planning of conversations can ignite thought-provoking interactions that can guide your practice.
2. Depending on the outcomes you seek, several kinds of conversations can be used to support your work.
3. Conversations for decision making are built upon investigative questions that expose, elaborate, and/or define specific information.
4. Well-crafted conversations with insightful questions produce opportunities to exchange knowledge and add to the collective wisdom of participants.
5. Conversations can and should be used to reflect, review, and reconsider ideas, thoughts, proposals, and decisions.
6. While we may enter into conversations for a variety of purposes, each conversation produces new understanding for participants.

Conversation Formats That Support Action Research Steps 2–4: Data Collection, Action Planning, and Plan Activation

So what have we learned so far? We have learned that oral inquiry conducted through purposeful conversations can be an effective tool in support of action research. We learned that conversations can help focus and refine the purpose of an action research project by generating a forum for the exchange of ideas. Whether your action research project is focusing on instructional decisions, gaining insight and feedback on practice, or attempting to deepen understanding of achievement results, wise use of conversations enriches your results.

You are now ready for step 2 of the model, conversation formats that support data collection and action planning for your action research project. These formats represent frames for the various kinds of communication you can use. You may notice that some concepts cross among the formats. This is purposeful, since the formats often are not applied alone but in tandem to address the complexities of classroom action research (Halliday 1993).

Cumulative Conversations

Cumulative conversations can sometimes resemble brainstorming sessions because they generate a continuous flow of ideas. Participants work together to produce a continuous stretch of supportive dialogue. Each comment or exchange extends the previous contributions of others.

You manage the process of this conversation format by asking questions or making suggestions to expand thinking or stimulate creativity. What this conversation yields is collections of ideas and possibilities. A reservoir of ideas like this can support and stimulate decision making and deepen understanding. This conversation format is an excellent way to start your investigation or gather insight before you make critical decisions about your project. You can use the following question stems to stimulate ideas with your mentor.

- What is working well?
- What are some reasons for this success?
- What evidence supports these reasons?
- What options are present?

Inferential Conversations

Sometimes your research needs may revolve around interpreting information, data, activities, or results. This is a complicated and conceptual task that requires skill in discriminating information, making inferences, and drawing conclusion from data. These conclusions formulate your perspective on the data. Engaging others in the analysis—colleagues to extend insight into possibilities, students to obtain insight into potential impact of those possibilities—provides an opportunity to not only expand the options available, but also extend your thinking and creativity. Thoughtful conversations woven into probing questions that peer into the data and generate storylines that help make sense of the information are the hallmark of this format.

This conversation format does not focus on generating ideas but rather on synthesizing ideas into conclusions that will drive your action. You will reach a point in your action research project when you will need to make sense of what is unfolding. Are you moving toward your target? Is the project doing what you expected? Probing questions like the sample stems that follow can be used with your mentor and colleagues in conversations to seek answers to those kinds of questions and concerns, or to make inferences and draw conclusions from your data.

- What does the data tell us about our work?

- How do the results reflect targets and/or goals?
- How well have we met expectations?
- What, if any, interventions are needed?

Exploratory Conversations

There comes a time in all action research projects when the rubber hits the road—the implementation of your design. If all is to go as expected and planned, all of the preparation—setting a purpose, analyzing the data, establishing a position with objectives and goals—would lead to a controlled and manageable process. Well, that result is more the exception than the rule. Consequently, you must be prepared to monitor and adjust as the project unfolds. This is where exploratory conversations can be very useful.

By monitoring the activities of the project, you can focus on current and topical issues surfacing within the process. For example, after a good start to your action research project with demonstrated results, your data begins to detect a small but consistent decrease in the activities that are producing your results. Is this a glitch in the process, a situation requiring change, or an anomaly? Then using "wondering questions" ("I wonder if . . . ?") with colleagues and students, you can ignite conversations that engage participants in creative thinking, new ideas, new goals, or new challenges.

By utilizing exploratory conversation, you create new choices and expand your potential to adjust your project to meet the challenges of a glitch or other implementation needs. In addition, you stimulate risk taking among staff and students. This grows confidence and will also stimulate thinking to question assumptions and seek new answers. What better foundation is there to underpin action research that seeks to make what we do better? Here are some sample question stems.

- I wonder about the impact of . . . ?
- What factors are contributing to the results we are achieving?
- What if we made these adjustments now? Later? When?
- How will we know if an adjustment is working?

Community-Building Conversations

There is much literature available that speaks to the importance of learning communities in our schools. Dufour et al. (2004) and the resiliency research of Henderson and Milstein (2002) stress the fact that these communities provide opportunities for continuous progress, something that is truly vital for the success of the teaching and learning process. Our action research has taught us that if our goal is to be better tomorrow than we are today and better next month than we are now, we must continue to question, continue to explore, and continue to learn. Underpinning this process is trust.

For any action research process to succeed—indeed, if any of the data that we gather from our project is to be valid—there must be a level of trust among all involved that what we are attempting to accomplish is something of value and meaning. Consequently, it is important to build trust among colleagues, students, and community. Conversations represent a powerful vehicle to accomplish this task.

Community-building conversations focus on engaging stakeholders in shared experiences. Open-ended questions that allow participants to share without critique can help increase understanding between the various groups that exist among stakeholders. Increasing understanding can in turn build trust. Building trust produces a solid foundation for your action research project. It is important to remember that we must begin to build trust early in the action research process. When you begin to plan your project, you can use one or more of these sample question stems to provide some focus to your thinking on who needs to be considered stakeholders in your project and how you can engage them to build your trust base.

- What are the expectations of this project?
- How can we accomplish these expectations?
- What criteria will we need to monitor progress?
- What roles and responsibilities are needed to address expectations?

**Checking for Understanding—Conversation Formats
That Support Action Research Steps 2–4: Data Collection,
Planning, and Implementation**
Things to remember:

1. Conversation formats are thinking frames that help you design conversation processes that manage the flow of information between and among participants.
2. Cumulative conversations are brainstorming sessions that yield collections of ideas and possibilities that extend the potential for new learning.
3. Inferential conversations are used to interpret information, make inferences, and draw conclusions. Probing questions are used to peer into the data to find the story.

4. Exploratory conversations help monitor and adjust the processes of action research. Using wondering questions ignites conversations that engage participants in creative thinking.

5. Community-building conversations focus energy on engaging all the stakeholders on the issues of importance. Open-ended questions increase the potential for deeper understanding and risk taking and can build trust.

Conversations Formats That Support Action Research Step 5: Outcome Assessment

In this phase of your action research, communication narrows and directs conversation into the data—what it is telling us, why it is what it is, and what needs to be done. These conversations are more structured than those in the first two steps of the model because they are actively engaged in defining what action is necessary to make an impact.

Conversation types are defined by specific question sequences aimed at gathering data that will be used to clear expectations. They are by nature analytical and pragmatic. The responsibility of these conversations is to establish benchmarks for action, set goals that are realistic and achievable, coach participants in the process by monitoring the activities within the project, and finally engage in the evaluation or assessment of the project. They are results oriented and push your thinking to answer quantitative and qualitative questions about your project: Did your project accomplish its goal? How do you track and measure your actions? What are the next steps? (Halliday 1993).

Benchmarking Conversations
Benchmarking conversations are important to the process because they provide opportunities to accomplish several things. First, they can be influential in establishing the current state or condition of teaching and learning in your classroom. This is critical to action because before you can set measurable and achievable goals, you have to know where you stand in current practice.

Benchmarking conversations can also be utilized after goals have been set to identify the parameters for how and when you measure your progress toward your goals. The conversations are driven by sequenced questions that peel away the unknown and expose the facts and details of practice. Benchmarking conversations produce a lot of data and ignite analytical exchanges that increase skill and competence in using information to guide practice. Notice the attention to evidence in the question stems that follow. They can provide a structure necessary to assess and set targets.

- What does the data tell us about current practice?
- What evidence exists to verify our position?
- Why is this evidence important?
- How will we measure progress?
- When do we need to stop and check our progress?
- What will we need to accurately identify progress or lack of progress as our project unfolds?

Goal-Setting Conversations

Goal-setting conversations are generally a combination of data review and risk-taking exercises. Usually they are experimental, or should we say mind stretching. They are important in helping establish the trajectory of your project and in motivating you and project participants to reach for that "brass ring." A word of caution here: there is a delicate balance that must be maintained within this type of conversation; remember, you are really setting the stage for your work.

When utilizing goal-setting conversations, you are establishing the end mark upon which you and your project will be evaluated. And through these conversations, you have shared and socialized these parameters with colleagues and students. Subsequently, you have made public the fundamental evaluative tools that measure your effort. As you might guess, this raises the stakes of these conversations and increases their importance within the construct of your project. Goal-setting conversations can and should use the collective wisdom of colleagues and also students in establishing targets.

The interchange within these goal-setting conversations should focus on identifying goals that are achievable and manageable. The input from others will provide some regulation and sculpting of the goals. These conversations are not as tied to data as the benchmark conversations, but they do need to keep the specifics of those benchmark conversations squarely in the sights as targets and goals are established.

The trademark of goal-setting conversations is the production of a forum for extending thinking and pushing the envelope of achievement. Goal-setting conversations are important to action research on many levels. Plan these conversations early with your mentor teacher and establish a timeline for reviewing your goals. The question stems that follow provide some direction for this review process.

- What level of performance will be achieved?
- What level of performance are we now?
- How do we move forward to our targets?
- How will we know we are making progress?

Coaching Conversations

Managing your action research project to success requires a process of continuous review and adjustment. Expecting the unexpected and handling shifts in the intermediate results that address each benchmark are simply part of the implementation process. In this environment, it is imperative that you maintain flexibility with options and that you have a pretty good understanding of what is transpiring.

Once again, conversations can provide valuable insight and support for this potentially contentious period of the project. Coaching becomes a viable methodology for this stage of your work. Relying on your mentor and colleagues to provide objective input and analysis, well-designed conversations can not only expand your perspective but also reinforce, reenergize, and perhaps refocus your thinking and your actions. Questions again are fundamental to these types of conversations. Reflective questions in particular can generate results that allow you to look objectively at your project through the eyes of those who are in a position to see the big picture and assist you in making what at times might be difficult decisions to shift or reconfigure some of the dynamics of the project.

Sometimes coaching conversations can also reinforce your thought process and provide you with a deeper understanding of what is unfolding and supporting the current path of action. Either way, these conversations must be built on accurate information and reviewed in an environment of trust. Your mentor and colleagues assume the role of "critical friend" in coaching conversations. Strategic use of questions like the stems below can provide an opportunity to learn from the insightful input of those critical friends. Perhaps even more important is the ability of these conversations to build resilient thinking and action to support your action research.

- What progress has been made?
- How have your actions supported or hindered the progress?
- Does the performance of the project meet the expectations set at the beginning of the project?
- What are the next steps that need to be taken to correct the trajectory and/or ensure success?

Assessment Conversations

Arguably the most important conversation type you will experience is the one that zeros in on the results of your action research project. It is important because the process of assessment is crucial to your project. How you design assessment, what you assess, and what you do with the assessment data impacts not only your evaluation of the project but also what you have learned and can use for further study. If you are strategic in your thinking, you can use assessment as a vehicle to evaluate, to learn, and to plan. If you are strategic in using conversations to guide your assessment process, you can gain insight into the human story that lies between the lines of data.

The reason you conduct action research is to perfect your craft, to teach and learn better. These are human aspirations as opposed to number targets. Conversations can increase participant engagement in the assessment process. Conversations will add the human perspective to the work by turning numbers into a story. The story brings meaning to the data and provides the opportunity for you to write new chapters to that story.

Remember, how you design your assessment process is important. Tap into those around you in the development stage of your project to focus on the data you will use to set goals and measure levels of success. Those conversations will set the stage for you to use one or more of the following sample stems to effectively analyze and assess your action research.

- What achievement level did you reach?
- What did you do or not do to generate those results?
- What would you do differently?
- What do the results tell you about your thinking and planning?
- What are the next steps?

Checking for Understanding—Conversation Types That Support Action Research Step 5: Outcome Assessment

Things to remember:

1. Conversation types are designed to focus the interventions of our practice. These conversations are structured, specific, and sequenced to provide clear expectations for learning and oriented for results.
2. Benchmarking conversations can establish the current state of your project and/or measure progress toward your goal. Their purpose is to set the pace for progress.
3. Goal-setting conversations are combinations of review and risk-taking activities. They establish the trajectory of your project and can motivate you to succeed. They are not as specific as benchmarking conversations, but they do use those targets to set goals.
4. Coaching conversations are used to monitor the progress of your project. During implementation, rarely does all go as planned. Coaching conversations help you obtain perspectives of your project other than

your own. These conversations build resiliency, expand knowledge and support creative problem solving.

5. Assessment conversations can impact what you have learned and how it can be used for further study. If you are strategic in using conversations to guide assessment, you can gain insight into the human story that lies between the lines of data you use to assess your project.

Practitioner's Corner

A unique feature of this chapter is this practitioner's corner. This section introduces focused voices from practice, sharing insight into the implementation of oral inquiry strategies in action research through two scenarios, one from an elementary teacher's perspective and another from a middle school teacher's view. The scenarios will demonstrate how various conversation formats or types are used to connect theory to practice.

So far in this chapter we have investigated oral inquiry strategies in action research that uses conversations as a methodology. We have examined conversations that can support the purpose of action research, and we have explored various conversation formats and styles to help us direct and focus thinking through benchmarking and goal setting and assessing. To help clarify how conversations can be used to support and enrich your research, the following reflections offer insight into how two teachers implemented the theory and concepts in their work with colleagues and students.

Practitioner's Corner 1: Middle School

Action research has been part of my ongoing teaching experience and a vital piece of my learning and growing as a teacher. Virtually all of my experience, which to date is two years, has been in middle school mathematics classrooms. For me, learning must be continuous and reflective, so I use the concepts and structure of action research to support my methodology. It has provided me a foundation for exploration and a reservoir of new learning that I can use to address student needs. Learning how to use conversations with teachers and especially with students, in action research, my learning reached levels I had not experienced before. Using planned conversations with students simply changed the learning experience.

I began my career in a middle school math classroom in a district that was struggling with success rates of their students. The district had never been successful on the state assessments due to significant problems with funding and support programs. In this caldron, I had to seek new ways of helping students learn. Even though I was using all of my pre-service learning, much of that learning did not provide insight into the demands of economically disadvantaged middle school students. I had to rely on my ability to use action research, and tap the knowledge of fellow teachers to address these real issues that confronted the learning process.

Because I was a new teacher confronted with significant issues in a struggling school, the knowledge and skills of fellow teachers were a constant pool of information for me. Learning how to use conversations to extract knowledge from colleagues was important. Knowing the different kinds of conversations that I could use to engage my colleagues helped me focus time and energy.

Most of the time in my action research, I used conversations that helped make decisions regarding interventions and exploratory conversations that helped us all look at what has been working and what has not. Even though some of what they shared had been unsuccessful, by engaging these teachers in conversations about students, my knowledge about the students grew. I think it also provided an opportunity for my colleagues to reflect on their craft. No matter, these conversations were important for me and for them, they brought us together, and they helped us share and produce common goals for all. The scores of our students rose steadily, so we knew that something was working, and through continuous reflective research we could refine and perfect those strategies that indeed were making a difference.

At the end of the 2007 school year, my position was eliminated, along with most secondary teaching positions, as the school district was reorganized. Subsequently, I found myself in a new situation. I was again teaching middle school math but in a new district. The environment had changed, but the challenges to student achievement were similar. Once again I was challenged with students who were struggling with mathematics and success on the state assessment. My new district, and my grade level in particular, had not demonstrated success in mathematics achievement. It was time for me to focus on what I knew and use my experience to carve an action plan.

It did not take long to make connections with my new colleagues. Our department was populated by eager teachers who had accepted the challenge presented by the student achievement record.

The first opportunity I had to engage in conversations with fellow teachers was during curriculum sessions in the summer. Developing curricula helped me engage in conversations that explored options and asked open-ended wondering questions along with very focused questions on the how and why of intervention strategies. This process helped me gain insight into the content and the methodologies that presented potential for increasing student achievement. As it turns out, this was very important learning for me. I learned much about the content and even more about my colleagues and the potential of my students.

Based upon what I had learned, I approached the year with optimism. For the most part, it started out well. The first few weeks were filled with good classroom dynamics. The students were participating.

Then the tide turned quickly and abruptly. Behavior changed, effort slacked, and students began to pull away. It was hard to tell what had caused the change. My thought was that we had crossed over a comfort barrier for the students. As new material increased in difficulty, the students' confidence lessened. I needed more information and I needed to reengage the students. At department meetings I engaged teachers in conversations that focused on developing a better understanding of the situation and the generation of decisions that would drive actions to adjust the current trend.

The conversations with colleagues produced a plan of action. That plan was to use the students' achievement data in conversations that would hold them accountable and responsible for their learning. These conversations would engage students in benchmarking, goal-setting, and assessment conversations about their work. It was a plan that would use conversations with students to guide and monitor an intervention.

I met with students individually in short, focused conversations where the students graphed achievement results and talked about their progress. These conversations engaged each student in discussing his or her effort and achievement; the results of these conversations were recorded in journals, and the effort of students was displayed on what I called a "power board."

Students became part of the intervention. The conversations helped me adjust strategies to meet the needs of individuals and groups of students. They produced an opportunity for students to get involved with their learning in a personal way. As a result, conversation became the "action" in my action research. I learned new ways of motivating students and helping them reach new levels of learning. In the process, student achievement also hit new levels and helped the school; the grade and the district achieved success on the state assessment. Truly a win-win situation.

Practitioner's Corner 2: Elementary

After three years in various teaching positions that included special education and general classroom assignments, I started a new position as a reading specialist in a new school district. I think my excitement was exceeded only by the anxiety of meeting several new challenges in a new community with new children. What helped keep me focused in this time of transition was the experiences I carried with me.

Throughout my tenure at my previous district, I used action research to help design the interventions within my classroom and in small study groups at grade level, with fellow teachers. I had learned strategies that provided insight into potential solutions to a lot of interconnected learning issues.

What I learned as well is that engaging colleagues and students in discussions and conversations about the issues we faced created a wonderful opportunity for everyone to participate in the process. This was really important because it bonded us all together—teachers, students, administrators, and community members. Through learning conversations, we began to see issues through common lenses. This really enhanced our thinking and generated solutions that incorporated the thoughts, ideas, and goals of many. It was a great learning experience for me.

In my new situation, I wanted to try to re-create that environment, but first there were several things I needed to do to set the stage for this new learning opportunity: I needed to learn more about my students, I needed to learn more about the staff that surrounded me, and I needed to know more about the school community and the parent support network to understand just what kinds of things I could use to meet the needs of struggling learners.

It was an important fact that time was short. My learning curve was steep, and I needed to be strategic in how I addressed my needs. Relying on what I had learned and the knowledge I was building about how conversations can make a difference, I engaged my colleagues in the lunchroom, at grade-level meetings, and during staff meetings—both the formal ones and the impromptu ones that occurred during free periods and those walks from the classroom to the car at the end of the day. For the most part, the initial conversations were for the purpose of sharing knowledge and gaining a deeper understanding of the issues.

It was important for me to understand how my students had achieved average and above-average grades in reading last year when they were functioning two levels below grade level now. How was achievement measured? What were the expectations of the students and their families? What had been attempted that demonstrated success? Exploratory conversations not only helped me learn about potential interventions but also gave me some insight into how the staff and the community in general perceived the issues. The research calls them "cumulative conversations," because they provide opportunities for participants to build upon each other's thoughts and generate a positive source of ideas that are interconnected and share common goals. I just refer to them as conversations that allowed me to learn about those who surrounded me. Their knowledge of children and the school community helped me focus my thinking and planning.

These conversations helped me build a small network of colleagues who focused on the students, their learning needs, and some interventions that may provide some solutions to the achievement puzzle we faced. Within this network of professionals, I tried to keep the conversations open and fueled by the contributions of the partici-

pants. This allowed me to absorb the thinking and learn more about the underlying principles that supported teaching and learning in the district.

I must say, in some of these conversations I was learning more about my colleagues and the community than about students and strategies. In that sense, the conversations helped me produce a disposition, a point of view, about my students and expectations. This was important because it helped me design interventions that had a real chance of succeeding because they reflected the belief system of students and parents. It was through these conversations that I learned that my students demonstrated behavior problems because they were really disconnected from the learning. They were careless in their approach, and for the first two years of their education were really passive participants. In most cases, there was little or no interaction that pushed them to think more deeply.

So, my challenge then was to construct new ways to involve the students. This was no easy task, because as I have mentioned the students were not used to getting involved. It was much easier for them to just do what they were told. After all, if they did this they received grades that were acceptable to them and their parents. It was a simple equation that everyone supported.

It became obvious that if I was going to succeed here I needed to engage the students in the process as well. The conversations needed to involve them in setting new expectations and in the goal-setting process that would help drive their new learning. This is where conversations with students became so important. Much to the surprise of many of my colleagues, our new network began to engage the students in looking at their own work.

Using the data that we gathered from classroom assessments and district monitoring assessments, I began to engage the students in benchmarking and goal-setting conversations. This held them accountable for their work. Through these daily conversations, we identified what they knew, why they knew it, and what should happen next. At times this was a difficult endeavor that required me to produce many questions and continue to pose these questions to guide student thinking.

Interestingly, however, after the students began to see just how much of a difference they could make in their own learning, the conversations became more natural. We were able to sit with students and have them make really good suggestions about their performance and set good achievable goals. The students were beginning to learn how to learn. They became active participants in their learning and vital pieces to my action research projects. Each new intervention for the students resulted from the information and insight gathered from students and colleagues. I watched some of my colleagues learn new strategies for interacting with students. I watched students learn new ways to communicate with teachers and each other. I learned new methods to support action research in my classroom.

Perhaps most important about this process was the learning that the parents and some of my colleagues experienced as well. The new accountability for students also produced new visions about what it took to be successful and what true success really was. Students, parents, and colleagues learned that past practices did not push students to think beyond expectations. The conversations provided me tremendous insight into how to think about and design interventions that could change the learning experience for students. These same conversations changed the way teachers and students thought about teaching and learning.

By the end of the year, all twenty-four students were reading at grade level, and a new set of expectations existed for students, parents, and our educational community. That speaks volumes for the impact of human conversations in the learning process.

Oral Inquiry Learning Conversation Template

In appendix A is a protocol you can use to structure your conversations with colleagues and students as you think about, plan, execute, and assess your action research project. The template will help you order and sequence your conversations and bring some format to the oral inquiry process. As you know, if conversations are to truly be oral inquiry, they must be purposeful, focused, and provide information that can be used to inform thinking and practice. This template provides that structure. Important to remember is the fact that this template can be used in any of the conversation formats and styles that you have learned about. So whether you are attempting to establish a purpose for your action research and using conversations to focus whether it should be a project that is seeking decisions on practice, or attempting to exchange information and grow knowledge or to deepen understanding of a particular issue that is impacting your practice, these templates can help in planning and implementing conversations that can make a difference. The template also can play a key role in the more focused conversations that establish benchmarks, monitor progress, and assess the impact of your project.

Putting the Pieces Together

Throughout this chapter, the process of oral inquiry through learning conversations has been explored. In an attempt to provide insight, the conversation model was presented in fragments, examining conversation purpose, formats, and types in isolated forums. This approach provided the opportunity to explore conversation methods and conversation methodology. The objective was to increase knowledge of how conversations can be used to support and enhance the five-step action research model you learned in chapter 1. The practitioner's corners that followed connected model design and theory to practice by sharing case scenarios demonstrating how an oral inquiry method of action research produced results for students. Finally, the conversation templates provide a structure for thinking and planning how to use conversations to support your action research project. Your challenge now is to conduct your own research and discover if engaging the human capital that surrounds you in learning conversations can bring you better results.

Questions for Review and Reflection

1. What assumptions of conversation strategies and/or action research were validated or challenged by contents of this chapter?
2. What implications does this have for your thinking and your practice?
3. What have you learned about question design and question strategies that will impact your thinking about action research?
4. How has the concept of conversation used as oral inquiry impacted your beliefs and/or assumptions of action research as a thinking and learning process?
5. What kind of words, phrases, and/or questions could you use in action research to do the following:
   (a) Brainstorm ideas
   (b) Interpret information and outcomes
   (c) Explore issues, possibilities, or solutions
   (d) Build trust and consensus among stakeholders in action research projects
6. What are the next steps in your learning that will enable you to use conversation strategies to support action research?

References

Dufour, R., R. Dufour, R. Eaker, and G. Karhanek. 2004. *Whatever it takes: How professional learning communities respond when kids don't learn.* Bloomington, IN: Solution Tree.

Halliday, M. A. K. 1993. *Towards a language-based theory of learning, linguistics, and education.* New York: Oxford University Press.

Henderson, N., and M. Milstein. 2002. *Resiliency in schools: Making it happen for students and educators.* Thousand Oaks, CA: Corwin Press.

Kanevsky, R. 1993. Descriptive review of a child: A way of knowing about teaching and learning. In *Inside/outside: Teacher research and knowledge*, ed. M. Cochran-Smith and S. Lytle. New York: Teachers College Press.

Kemmis, S., and R. McTaggart. 1988. *The action research planner*. 3rd ed. Victoria, Australia: Deakin University Press.

Moll, L., ed. 1990. *Vygotsky and education: Instructional implications and applications of sociohistorical psychology*. New York: Cambridge University Press.

Vygotsky, L. 1962. *Thought and language*. Cambridge, MA: MIT Press.

Wertsch, J. 1991. *Voices of the mind: A sociocultural approach to mediated action*. Cambridge, MA: Harvard University Press.

Appendix A: Action Research Oral Inquiry Template

Table 1 Establishing Conversation Purpose to Support Action Research Step 1 Issue Identification

Establishing a Purpose for Action Research Project	
Conversations that support purpose	**Applications/scenarios**
Sharing Knowledge Conversations	1. Working with your mentor(s) to identify potential topics for your Action Research Project
	2. Attempting to describe or define topics of interest
	3. "Brainstorming" ideas (cumulative conversation)
Gaining Understanding Conversations	1. Reflecting upon the ideas generated through shared knowledge
	2. Examining and/or comparing ideas from mentor(s) and colleagues
	3. Gathering input and/or seeking support for your Action Research Project – (Community Building)
Decision-Making Conversations	1. Narrowing options and/or eliminating topics for consideration
	2. Examining evidence and data that supports various options/topics
	3. Establishing a clear focus/purpose to initiate action research project

Table 2 Conversation Formats That Support Action Research Steps 2–4, Data Collection, Action Planning, and Plan Activation

Design and Construction of Acion Research Project	
Conversations that support purpose	**Applications/scenarios**
Cumulative Conversations	1. Brainstorming strategies for implementation of Action Research Project
	2. Clarifying questions and ideas related to Action Research activities and interventions
	3. Gathering input from stakeholders on how the Action Research will operate
Inferential Conversations	1. Examining data for focusing need and/or designing interventions with best potential for meeting needs
	2. Estimating the resources and materials necessary to drive Action Research Project
	3. Projecting the potential scope and impact of Action Research Project
	4. Examining data from existing Action Research to determine what If any action is required
Exploratory Conversations	1. Planning for implementation of Action Research
	2. Constructing the What, How, Why, and When of Action Research Project
	3. Establishing the sequence of events that will drive and/or monitor Action Research Activity
	4. Review, examine, reflect on current Action Research activities and/or results

Conversation Types That Clear Expectations and Support Action Research Step-Assessment Outcomes

Implementation of Action Research Project	
Conversations that support purpose	**Applications/scenarios**
Benchmarking Conversations	1. To identify current levels of practice or current situations that Are related to Action Research Project
	2. To establish performance targets that will drive Action Research
	3. To establish the specific criteria that will provide data to monitor Actions toward targets—Clear Expectations for Project
	4. To Review progress toward the performance goals

Implementation of Action Research Project	
Conversations that support purpose	**Applications/scenarios**
Goal-setting Conversations	1. To establish the target goal the Action Research Project will achieve
	2. To identify the specific criteria that will be used to measure success
	3. To define how progress will be measured and what that progress means for the Action Research Project
Coaching Conversations	1. In sharing knowledge—to exchange perceptions of Action Research Project
	2. In gaining understanding process to gather insight into the How, Why, When, and What of Action Research Project
	3. In inferential process to help examine and interpret data important to the Action Research Project
	4. In exploratory process to examine issues that may be impacting Action Research Project
	5. In benchmarking process to examine current status of activities
	6. In goal-setting process to review targets and/or adjust actions
Assessment Conversations	1. To establish impact of Action Research Project on identified targets
	2. To identify what worked in the project and why, or what did not work and why
	3. To provide an overall evaluation of the Action Research Project And process

❦

CHAPTER SEVEN

Tools for Collaboration in Action Research

Ellen E. Ballock

As you have read in previous chapters, there are many data available to you as an action researcher to inform your reflective practice. Collaboration with other professionals (your peers, university supervisors, mentors, grade-level teams, paraprofessionals, specialists) through reflective conversation provides you with yet another data stream that you may find useful throughout your action research, from your initial issue identification all the way through your outcome assessment.

The purpose of this chapter is to help you enhance your action research through meaningful and effective collaboration with others. This chapter will guide you through the process of forming an action research community within your school. It will also equip you with tips for using three tools, called protocols, that you can use to structure effective and focused use of time within your action research community.

As you read, you will find examples of how these collaborative structures have led action researchers to a deeper understanding of their students, improved professional decision making, and greater clarity of thinking throughout the action research process.

Chapter Objectives

By the time you finish reading and thinking about this chapter you will be able to do the following:

- Identify benefits of collaboration during the action research process
- Establish your own action research community
- Recognize the role that structured conversational protocols play in facilitating focused and productive collaboration
- Identify the ways three specific protocols might support you through the various phases of your own action research process

Why Collaboration?

Effective teaching is difficult. It usually requires information, expertise, and support far beyond the resources available to the individual teacher working alone in an isolated classroom (Newmann 1994, 1).

The truth of the above quote will likely become more and more real for you throughout your entire teaching career. Teaching is complex. Often, you may ponder many questions or dilemmas connected with teaching, curriculum, and students. Perhaps you are facing concerns regarding your students' performance on a recent benchmark test because you feel their test scores do not match the level of mastery you observed in class. Maybe you are struggling to figure out what will motivate your learners or to solve a classroom management issue. Left to struggle with these concerns in silent isolation, you will likely feel increasingly uncertain, incompetent, and cynical.

On the other hand, taking the risk to share these questions and concerns and reflect-in-action in a collaborative manner with others—members of your grade-level team, or other professional educators within your school community—will allow you to transform struggles into opportunities for learning for you, your colleagues, *and* your students.

Developing an Action Research Community

Participating in an action research community is one way you can reap the benefits of professional collaboration during the action research process (Yendol-Hoppey and Dana 2009). This type of community consists of professional educators who share a commitment to intentional learning and problem solving through engaging in ongoing cycles of action research, and they commit to meeting together regularly to support each other in the action research process.

As a member of an action research community, you know that you have a safe space for sharing your deepest questions and concerns about teaching and about your students because that is your common purpose. In joining this type of community, you gain more than an emotional support group or a place to vent. Taking part in this community multiplies the resources available to you in your action research as you draw on the perspectives, expertise, and experiences of others in the community and work together to take action to solve problems.

Formulating Your Community

It is important when forming an action research community to identify other individuals who are willing to make a commitment to meet regularly for reflection in action. Although these communities can range in size, you will find four to twelve participants to be the ideal. This ensures that you will have access to many different perspectives during the action research process, while still maintaining time and space for all members to actively participate in conversation.

Consider developing an action research community with members of your grade level team or with a variety of professionals from within the school. Consider meeting with the other teachers in your school weekly or biweekly to support each other in the action research process. You can also talk with your local university professors about whether it would be possible to put together a community that includes teacher candidates, mentor teachers, and supervisors. You will find that each participant in such a mixed group really does bring a unique set of observations, questions, skills, and expertise to contribute to the community as a whole, helping you gain a broad range of perspectives on your action research.

If you are new to teaching, you might initially feel intimidated to share your questions or ideas in a group that includes experienced teachers, but try to remember that all participants in the community come as both learners and contributors, no matter where they are in their professional journey. You will be pleasantly surprised at how eager veteran teachers can be to contribute to your learning and how much your questions and contributions allow them to continue to reflect on their own teaching practice.

Establishing Community Norms

When your action research community meets for the first time, spend some time developing a set of norms for your community. Norms define expectations for group membership and participation based on the shared values of the group members. Norms govern our actions and attitudes in most social interactions, but often these norms are unstated. For example, you will not find a list of stated guidelines or expectations in the teachers lounge, but you will probably observe different types of behaviors and social interactions in that space than in staff meetings because individuals are operating by a different set of norms. Establishing norms more explicitly can be helpful as you start a new community to ensure that your community will operate purposefully. The norms you create for your action research community should support the intellectual work of professional discussion and problem solving.

Think about the process of developing norms as similar to involving students in developing classroom rules at the beginning of the school year. Collaboratively developing classroom expectations gives students a shared understanding and sense of ownership for the classroom learning environment. Similarly, spending time talking with your action research community about your hopes and expectations for your work together will help you develop a shared sense of purpose and ownership for the guidelines that will help your community function.

Norms vary, depending on the needs and interests of the specific action research community. For example, a community's members might agree on a short and simple list of norms, such as (1) Step up. (2) Make space. (3) Assume goodwill. Another community might agree to a slightly longer list of norms to guide their work: (1) Suspend judgment. (2) Take risks. (3) Include everyone as an equal. (4) Begin and end on time. (5) Maintain confidentiality. (6) When it's over, it's over. Each community is different, so each community's norms will be unique. The point is to establish common expectations to ensure that you are able to best support each other as action researchers. As you talk with your group about the norms that will best work for you, use the following questions as a guide:

- How often will you meet and how long will your meetings last?
- What responsibilities should group members have to each other?
- Is it OK for individuals to skip meetings? For what reasons?
- How will you maintain confidentiality?
- How will you each monitor your own participation so that everyone has opportunity for floor time?
- Will there be time for social talk or venting in your meetings? How much?
- How will you give open and honest feedback to one another without judging or criticizing each other?
- How will you handle conflict?

Your goal by the end of the conversation is to come to consensus on three to five statements that reflect the shared values and expectations that will guide your community's work. Record these statements on chart paper or poster board so that you can post them every time your group meets. However, do not feel as if you are stuck with these norms forever. You can always come back to update or adjust your group norms to meet the changing needs of your group over time.

Using Protocols as Tools to Focus Meetings

Unfortunately, not every conversation or collaborative grouping serves to improve teaching and learning within a school (Dufour et al. 2006). If the conversations within an action research community are to serve as a data stream to support reflection in action, then it is important not to leave the content of those conversations to chance. Members of effective action research communities find that protocols help them make the most of their meeting times. Protocols are tools for structuring conversations that are designed to enhance the productive focus of collaborative interactions. They provide a step-by-step outline for systematically addressing problems, sharing perspectives, or analyzing data.

Protocols also support helpful and productive patterns of group interaction. Have you ever approached friends or colleagues for help with a question or problem, only to find that they were so quick to jump in and share their own experiences and advice that they were unable to really hear and understand what you were trying to say? Have you ever participated in group meetings where conversations got so far off track that nothing got accomplished? Have you ever felt frustrated when a domineering group member stifled your own voice and perspective or, conversely, when no one else in the group seemed interested in stepping up to contribute?

Using protocols helps temper these ineffective social norms. The various steps in each protocol will serve to slow down your normal patterns of response, encouraging your community members to look more deeply at an issue, to ask questions rather than jump to conclusions, to look for evidence rather than just sharing opinions, and to seek out the perspectives of all participants in the group (Blythe, Allen, and Powell 1999).

Using protocols can feel a little awkward the first few times you try it, but as the processes become more familiar, new patterns of healthy group interaction begin to emerge that allow the members of your group to gain deeper insights through effective communication and focused use of time. For this reason, protocols work best when the participants have committed to meeting together regularly to support each other in their ongoing professional learning, such as in an action research community. To experience a virtual protocol, you can check out the Looking at Student Work website monitored by the National School Reform Faculty: www.lasw.org/vp.html.

Common Protocol Features

Organizations such as the National School Reform Faculty, the Coalition for Essential Schools, and Harvard's Project Zero have developed protocols that can support action research and teacher learning in schools. Though each protocol serves a unique purpose, there are a number of features that are common across protocols. Understanding these commonalities will serve as helpful background for considering specific protocols you may want to use during your own cycles of action research.

First, there are three roles you and the other members of your community would typically take during a protocol: facilitator, presenter, and participant. The facilitator of a protocol is responsible for opening the meeting by introducing the presenter and the selected protocol, ensuring that the group stays focused, keeping track of time, and helping move the group from one protocol step to the next. The presenter is the individual who prepares the focus question, data, or artifact that the group will discuss during the protocol. In contrast to other settings in which the presenter conveys information and expertise to an audience, the presenter in a protocol comes ready to learn, seeking new insights and perspectives from the group's discussion. There are usually six to eight other participants in the protocol. These individuals do not need to prepare anything in advance. They simply show up ready to think deeply and discuss their observations and interpretations according to the steps laid out in the protocol.

A second feature you will frequently notice in protocols is a period of time in which the presenter is a silent observer of the discussion rather than an active participant. During this time participants do not direct their comments to the presenter, but rather talk about the question or artifacts among themselves as if the presenter is not even there. The presenter may even pull a chair aside to sit outside the participant circle. Though this practice may strike you as odd, there are important benefits to the presenter. First, it protects the presenter. The following entry from a new action researcher's journal entry provides insight into why this is important:

> Being a presenter is a very personal experience. . . . I believe that when you present material of your own you have so much of a personal bias that it is hard to let go and just receive constructive feedback. I know that I have strong feelings for my students and I care about them deeply when I work with them in the classroom. In saying this, I know that by having these feelings I am very emotionally charged in the group setting because I feel like I am the only one who would be able to remedy the situation by taking the ideas of others and then tweaking them to fit *my* students, because no one could possibly have students like mine.

They may think they do but they couldn't. This type of attitude is something that I noticed of myself through my presentation. (L.S., 2008)

As you can see from the above passage, being a presenter is sometimes a very personal and emotional experience. In such a case it is easy to become defensive. A defensive attitude, however, inhibits your ability to listen, consider alternate viewpoints, or learn from others. Stepping back to listen in silence grants you an emotional buffer. Rather than thinking about how to defend yourself or your students or further clarify the specifics of the problem, you have the opportunity to simply listen to what others have to say, reflectively weighing the value of others' perspectives for your specific case.

This next journal entry explains how another intern found it beneficial to just listen to the group discuss, even if some of what the participants talked about did not seem applicable at the time:

The next part was the hardest for me. The group had their turn to think of possible assessment plans and I couldn't participate in the discussion. I made sure to write down everything, even if I didn't particularly like the idea. The group brought up many good points along with some creative plans of action. Sometimes I wouldn't like the idea as a whole, but I would see parts of the idea that could be useful. (S.A., 2008)

The opportunity to just listen without any pressure to respond allowed this action researcher the space to really reflect on what other participants said and to sort through which perspectives and suggestions might best make sense in her own classroom setting.

The third feature common across the protocols we will explore is a time of debriefing at the end. During this protocol step, participants separate themselves from the content of the conversation in which they have been engaged and take a few minutes to talk about the actual process of going through the protocol. Focusing on the experience of going through the protocol will allow your action research community to become more comfortable with using protocols as tools for structuring conversation. It will also allow you to consider whether there are ways you would like to tweak the protocol or your use of the protocol for the future. You might discuss questions such as the following:

How did this process work for us today?
How did the process help or hinder us in what we set out to accomplish today?
What did you like/dislike about the process?
What should we improve in our group process for the future?

Three Protocols to Support Your Action Research

The remainder of this chapter highlights three specific protocols you may find useful during the action research process: the descriptive consultancy protocol, the collaborative assessment protocol, and the data driven dialogue protocol. Figure 7.1 serves as a quick reference to help you compare these three protocols, while the descriptions that follow will help you further distinguish between the unique purposes of each protocol. This section will also provide you with both an example of how each of these protocols has been used to support action research and tips for getting the most out of using each specific tool.

The Descriptive Consultancy Protocol: Action Research as Problem Solving

Often your impetus for action research will be a perceived problem or issue that arises within your classroom or school practice, and any issue that is significant enough to warrant an intentional action research process will probably be complex and messy. Simply asking your colleagues for advice on addressing such issues may not be as helpful as you hope because you may find it difficult to even identify the heart of the issue, and any suggested quick fixes will likely be insufficient for addressing a complex problem.

When you find that you need help to think more expansively about an issue so that you can more clearly define a problem and identify some possible cause-and-effect relationships at work within the problem, using the descriptive consultancy protocol (Mohr, no date) with your action research community will serve you well. This protocol is most often used toward the beginning of the five-step action research process identified in chapter 1. It can help you more clearly identify and understand the problem and articulate

Figure 7.1. Protocols for action research.

Protocol	Purpose	Roles in the action research process
Descriptive consultancy	Thinking more expansively about a problem or an issue	Issue identification Action planning
Collaborative assessment	Learning about a student through looking at a piece of student work	Issue identification Action planning Outcomes assessment
Data-driven dialogue	Making inferences and drawing conclusions based on a close observation of data Developing a shared meaning of data	Data analysis for: Issue identification Outcome assessment

the research question during the issue identification phase, and the pos-sible next steps participants generate can support you with action planning. However, you may also find it useful at any point during the process if you feel stuck, because the perspectives from others can provide fresh insights, encouragement, and possibilities for next steps. Figure 7.2 outlines the steps involved in this protocol. These steps include an opportunity for you as the presenter to describe the problem, for participants to ask you questions and discuss the problem, and for you to respond to the discussion.

Let's take a look at how a teacher candidate made use of the descriptive consultancy protocol. Mark felt consistently challenged in working with one particular student in his second-grade classroom, a student who excelled academically but frequently distracted himself and other students with his behaviors. Mark decided to use the descriptive consultancy protocol during a meeting with his action research community to help him think in new ways about working with this student.

Descriptive Consultancy Protocol

Developed by Nancy Mohr

Estimated Time: 30–35 minutes

1. The presenter describes the issue or the problem in detail to the group. Par-ticipants listen and take any notes they perceive may be helpful. *(5 minutes)*
2. Participants ask clarifying questions. These questions require only brief factual answers and help participants make sure they are clear on what the presenter has said. *(2–3 minutes)*
3. Participants describe what they have heard the presenter say about the issue, seeking to develop a shared understanding of the issue's complexi-ties. What did we hear? What didn't we hear that we need to know more about? What questions arise for us? *The presenter is silent during this time. (5–7 minutes)*
4. The presenter responds to the group's discussion, providing additional infor-mation needed to clarify the group's description of the issue. *(3–4 minutes)*
5. Participants discuss the issue, brainstorming possible causes, identifying potential next steps, and suggesting possible solutions. *The presenter is silent during this time. (7 minutes)*
6. The presenter responds, highlighting what was potentially useful from the group's discussion and articulating possible next steps to take. *(3–4 minutes)*
7. The entire group debriefs the protocol. *(5 minutes)*

Figure 7.2.

In going through the steps of this protocol, his fellow interns and university supervisor helped him consider multiple possible causes for this student's behaviors: (1) lack of clarity as to the classroom rules and consequences, (2) lack of interest or motivation in lessons, and (3) a desire for attention. They also suggested a number of possible interventions or action steps for working to better support this student's classroom participation and learning. New perspectives on the issue allowed Mark to think more clearly about the specific kinds of data he would want to collect to better define the problem so that he could craft a focused research question and identify appropriate strategies or interventions. In a written reflection following this protocol, Mark wrote that the protocol "allowed me to quit complaining and get to the heart of the issue at hand—to put everything to the side and make sure that the learner's needs are addressed."

It is important to emphasize two points that helped make this protocol session such a positive experience for Mark. First, Mark prepared in advance for this meeting. He spent time thinking about the issue he wanted the group to discuss and made notes to help him remember the points he wanted to emphasize. This allowed him to clearly explain the issue as he understood it to the other participants. Mark's preparation allowed the group to make the best use of their time. Second, participants in this protocol monitored their own contributions to the discussion. They kept in mind that their purpose was not necessarily to fix the problem, but to try to examine the issue from many angles. They also chose to keep their conversation focused on Mark's experiences with this specific student rather than spending the time talking about their own frustrations with students in their own classrooms. Though all participants left the meeting with new thoughts to mull over in regard to their own classroom situations, they realized that during this particular protocol their primary purpose was to provide support to Mark.

The Collaborative Assessment Protocol: Learning from Student Work during Action Research

If there is one thing you are probably beginning to feel familiar with as you take over teaching responsibilities during the course of your internship, it is looking at student work. You may be feeling surprised or overwhelmed by the number of hours each week that you spend providing students with feedback on their work, grading homework and class work, and using student work to inform your instructional decisions.

As an action researcher, you will find that student work is a critical data source. Tracking student scores on class work, tests and quizzes, and other assessments provides you with quantitative data that will help you monitor student achievement and draw conclusions about the relative success of instructional strategies or interventions you try. There will also be times during your action research process when you will need to really get at the meaning behind those scores through a deeper and more sustained qualitative analysis of student work samples.

The purpose of the collaborative assessment protocol, developed by Steve Seidel and Harvard's Project Zero, is to guide your group through a focused analysis of one piece of student work in order to learn more about the student, how the student might be thinking, and where the student is in the learning process (Blythe, Allen, and Powell 1999). You might use this protocol toward the beginning of your action research process to help you with issue identification, or you might use it to support your ongoing data analysis during plan activation and outcome assessment. Figure 7.3 highlights the steps in this protocol, including observation, description, asking questions, speculation, and discussion of implications for teaching and learning.

Let's look at how one social studies teacher used this protocol to help her address her action research question: "How can I support students in deeper levels of thinking and meaning making in social studies?" Eileen asked the teachers in her cross-disciplinary action research community to join her in a collaborative assessment protocol looking at a research project her students had completed on a hero or heroine from American history. This project represented the culmination of instruction intentionally focused on helping students go beyond just the facts to deeper thinking and meaning making by helping them develop skills in questioning and making inferences. Although there was a range of quality in the assignments students turned in, she was very pleased with the overall thinking and meaning making she felt she saw in the projects. However, she wondered what her colleagues would see in the projects that would help her understand her students and where they were in their learning even more deeply. She writes:

> When I've participated in this protocol before, the presenter usually had a really specific reason for selecting a particular child's work sample (though they did not share that reason with the group at first). However, for this project I did not have a specific student I was concerned about. I was more interested in selecting a work sample that might represent my class as a whole, so I decided to bring a project sample of average quality based on the grades students had received on the project. As we began, I worried about whether my colleagues' perspectives would give me anything new to think about, since they are not social studies teachers and therefore don't know social studies content or goals as well as I do. There was no need for that! Hearing them discuss this work sample was so good in that it both reaffirmed what I felt I had seen while also giving me new things to think about.

Collaborative Assessment Protocol

Developed by Steve Seidel and colleagues at Project Zero

Estimated Time: 45 minutes minimum

1. Looking at student work: The presenter provides a copy of the selected student work sample *(with student name or other identifiers removed)* to each participant, but does not provide any context or background information about the piece of work. *(The presenter does not speak until step 5.)* Participants read and make notes to themselves about the work in silence. *(5 minutes)*
2. Describing student work: Participants share concrete observations and descriptions of what they see in the work without making judgments about the quality of the work. The facilitator asks for evidence to back up a judgment if any does emerge. *(5 minutes)*
3. Asking questions about student work: Participants share the questions that the piece of student work raises for them, perhaps about the assignment, about the specific student, or about the teaching and learning process involved. The presenter may choose to take notes on these questions but does not answer them at this time. *(5 minutes)*
4. Speculating about student work: Participants share their thoughts about what knowledge, skills, or dispositions they think the specific student may be working on based on their observations of the student work. They speculate as to problems or issues the student may have focused on while working on the assignment and what the student may have felt was important in successfully completing the assignment. The presenter takes notes on ideas that stand out. *(5 minutes)*
5. Hearing from the presenter: The presenter responds, sharing his or her perspective about the student work, possibly addressing some of the questions from step 3, and highlighting what stood out as surprising or potentially useful from the group's description, questions, and speculations. *(5 minutes)*
6. Discussing implications for teaching and learning: Everyone (presenter and all other participants) has the opportunity to share thoughts about ways to support this particular student in future instruction as well as what broader implications there might be for teaching and learning in their own classrooms with their own students. *(15 minutes)*
7. Debriefing the protocol. *(5 minutes)*

Figure 7.3.

Without Eileen's even asking for specific feedback on student thinking and meaning-making, participants in this protocol noticed that the research project went beyond the facts to include inferences, connections between the hero's life and the historical context, and connections to the student's own life. These observations helped validate Eileen's perceptions of quality in student work, but also helped give her some more specific language for explaining why the projects represented quality thinking, enabling her to draw stronger conclusions based on her action research. This protocol also raised new thoughts and questions for Eileen. For example, one of the project requirements was to include a visual component to represent the significance of the hero. After listening to her colleagues' observations and questions about this project component, she reflected:

> I know that my expectation for creating a visual for this project is more than making a "craft." It's my expectation that the visual would communicate meaning just like a piece of writing is intended to communicate meaning. However, I never explicitly explained that to students. The expectation was that all components of the project would exhibit depth of thought, connection to context, and creativity; but I wonder if my students, like me, can more easily envision that in written genres than in art or visuals . . . Having conversations about what visuals can mean and how they communicate would be really beneficial.

Using this protocol both confirmed conclusions Eileen was beginning to make about her students' thinking and gave her new questions and directions to pursue with her research question.

Several factors contributed to the success of this protocol. The first was Eileen's selection of student work. Eileen knew that selecting an open-ended assignment, such as her student research projects, would allow for a richer experience with this protocol than more closed-ended assignments, such as multiple choice tests or drills. When an answer is either right or wrong, there is little to observe and discuss about the work sample. In contrast, open-ended assignments allow for a window into students' thought processes, skill development, and understandings that can provide the basis for fruitful discussion. Writing samples, projects, problem-solving exercises, and artwork are a few other examples of the type of open-ended assignments that work well with the collaborative assessment protocol.

The participants played a crucial role in the success of this protocol. Often the biggest initial challenge for participants in this protocol comes during what seems like the most basic of steps: describing the student work. Since teachers are used to making quick judgments about student work, distinguishing concrete observations from evaluations of the work takes practice. Describing the work using concrete observations often feels like stating the obvious. For example, "I see that a paragraph, a picture, and a chart have been used to display information in this report" or "I see ten adjectives in this paragraph." In contrast, evaluating student work attaches some sort of value to the work—for example, "The picture in this report sure is sloppy" or "This student really does a great job of using descriptive language." While describing concrete features of the student work may feel very basic and unnecessary, participants who discipline themselves to focus on description rather than evaluation in this protocol step are often able to gain deeper insights from the remaining protocol steps than if they immediately jumped into evaluating the work.

The Data-Driven Dialogue Protocol: Diving into Data Analysis

Data plays a critical role in your action research process, whether it is baseline data that helps prompt the initial issue identification or action planning, or data collected and analyzed in an ongoing manner during plan activation and outcome analysis. Collecting the data is the easy part. Making sense of the data is more of a challenge. Often, the inferences you draw are influenced by your past experiences, beliefs, and assumptions.

Novice researchers often use data simply to confirm their prior beliefs or expectations. For example, an action researcher who feels comfortable using a specific reading program might look at the data with an eye toward proving that the reading program really is effective rather than looking for gaps in student learning that result from using the program. To avoid this trap and truly make good use of your data, it will be important to separate your hopes, beliefs, and assumptions about the data from what the data actually says, so you can best use it to inform your work as a teacher.

The purpose of the data-driven dialogue protocol (Teacher Development Group 2002) is to support you as a researcher in setting aside your assumptions in order to take a closer look at what the data is really telling you. This will allow you to draw more valid conclusions and to make the most appropriate decisions for serving your learners.

The data-driven dialogue protocol supports a group of collaborative researchers in developing a shared understanding of a common data set. This protocol works well for examining classroom assessment data, schoolwide standardized test scores, or even district-level data. You can also use this protocol to examine survey results, interview responses, field notes, or any other data source that is pertinent to your action research question. You might use this protocol at the beginning of your action research to assess baseline data, during your middle stages to assess formative data, or at the end of your research to determine what you have learned as a result of doing your action research. Figure 7.4 lays out the steps for this protocol.

The following example depicts how Ethan's issue identification came as a direct result of using the data-driven dialogue protocol with his eighth-grade team.

The school in which Ethan was placed for his internship was focused on supporting reading comprehension in the content areas of science and social studies as part of the school improvement plan for the year. During a team meeting, Ethan's team was charged with the task of looking at standardized test scores and student grades to identify students who would benefit from targeted support in content area reading. The assumption was that students performing below grade level on the reading portion of the state's standardized test would need the most support with reading in the content areas.

Ethan's team decided to use the data-driven dialogue protocol to help them take a broader look at what the data might tell them about student achievement in the content areas. As they analyzed the data, they were able to identify specific students to target with extra support in reading as they

---

Data-driven Dialogue Protocol

Developed by the Teacher Development Group

Estimated Time: 40 minutes

1. Introduction: The presenter briefly explains what kind of data the group will be looking at without actually passing it out or providing any interpretations of the data.
2. Predictions: Participants begin by silently thinking about their own prior experiences and assumptions about what they think will be seen in the data using thought stems, such as I assume... I predict... I wonder.... Participants then share their predictions, the factors from their prior experiences that influence these predictions, and talk about what possibilities for learning there might be in actually looking at the data.
3. Observations: Participants take time to silently look through the data, making notes about only the facts using thought stems, such as I observe... I can count... A pattern/trend I notice is... I'm surprised to see.... Participants then share their observations without making any interpretations or drawing any conclusions yet.
4. Inferences: Participants silently reflect on what the data might mean using thought stems, such as The data suggests ____ because... Additional data that would help to verify or confirm this is... Appropriate solutions or next steps based on this data might be... Additional data that would guide implementation of these next steps is.... Participants then discuss these inferences and explanations.
5. Debrief the protocol.

Figure 7.4.

had been charged, but that was not the most important outcome of the meeting. They also discovered in analyzing the data that many more boys than girls were earning Ds and Fs in social studies. They were even more surprised when they noticed that many of these same male students scored at or above grade level in both reading and math on the standardized test. This seemed to suggest that reading comprehension was not the only issue interfering with student achievement.

Throughout the rest of the week the members of Ethan's team discussed many competing explanations for why these specific students were not succeeding: lack of motivation, poor study skills, over-involvement in intramural sports, too much interest in winning the attention of the girls in class, and so forth. They also expressed many strong and varied opinions as to how to improve achievement for their male students. However, without a means of gathering and examining additional data, these teachers could not come to consensus as to the root of the problem or what strategies they should implement.

With the backing of his team, Ethan began his action research project investigating the factors affecting the achievement of their male students. He collected numerous forms of data, one of which was a survey he gave to all the eighth-grade boys. This survey included questions about extracurricular activities, students' interests, career aspirations, attitudes towards school, and a learning styles inventory (Sternberg and Gigorenko 2000).

Ethan and his team then used the data-driven dialogue protocol once more in order to take a look at the survey data. During the process they realized that, according to the learning styles portion of the survey, a commonality among their underachieving male students was high scores for creative thinking but fairly low scores for analytical thinking. This seemed to fit with an observation Ethan had made when looking at these students' grades when he noticed a pattern of low scores on tests and homework, but higher grades on projects.

As Ethan's team reflected on the instruction and assessment practices typical in eighth-grade social studies, they realized that reading about history, memorizing key dates and facts, and analyzing historical events dominated their practice. After reflecting on the data and their teaching practice, Ethan and the other social studies teachers decided to make two important adjustments to the next social studies unit. First, they brainstormed ways to more explicitly support students in developing the analytical thinking skills historians use to understand the past so students could experience greater success with these types of tasks. Second, they developed new assessment tasks involving creative thinking that would allow creative thinkers to use their strengths and other learners to grow in the area of creative thinking.

Ethan and his team allowed themselves to be surprised by their data. Using this protocol to look at standardized test scores and student grades in the first team meeting helped them look for patterns and connections they might not have naturally thought to consider. The outcome was a data-driven action research project focused on issues affecting student achievement. Using this protocol in the second team meeting then allowed this team of teachers to leave behind their differing and conflicting assumptions about their underachieving male students, to develop a common understanding of an issue affecting these boys' achievement, and to make better decisions about how to address the issues in their teaching practice.

It is unlikely that you would use the data-driven dialogue protocol to replace your own individual data analysis process during action research. However, as a beginning researcher, this protocol can provide you with some initial support so that data analysis does not feel so foreign or overwhelming; and for researchers of any level of experience, the opportunity to hear the perspectives of others allows for a deeper and more thorough analysis of the data from which to draw conclusions.

Final Thoughts

Educational researchers have found that when members of a school faculty collaborate, not just by sharing exemplary lesson plans with each other, but by engaging in the intellectual work of professional learning and problem solving, the result is continuous school improvement: Teachers are better able to change their teaching practice to meet the needs of their students and student achievement increases (e.g., Little 1982; McLaughlin and Talbert 1993, 2006; Wheelan and Kesselring 2005).

In this chapter you have read examples of how professional collaboration within the context of the action research process has led to improvements in teaching and student learning. You have read about the role that protocols played in facilitating collaboration. You have also read about how implementing these protocols led individuals to reflect thoughtfully and take meaningful action in their teaching practice. Now your challenge is to consider how you can work collaboratively with others in a process of ongoing professional learning. Spend some time reflecting on the closing questions to help you get started.

Questions for Review and Reflection

1. How do structures such as community norms and protocols facilitate effective collaboration?

2. With whom might you meet to form an action research community?
3. What norms would you want to see guiding your community's work?
4. Which of the three protocols discussed best fits with your current stage of action research? What question, dilemma, student work sample, or data might your colleagues help you consider? The flowchart for protocol decision making in appendix A will help you determine which protocol you feel most ready to try.

References

Blythe, T., D. Allen, and T. S. Powell. 1999. *Looking together at student work*. New York: Teachers College Press.

Dufour, R., R. Dufour, R. Eaker, and T. Many. 2006. *Learning by doing: A handbook for professional learning communities at work*. Bloomington, IN: Solution Tree.

Little, J. W. 1982. Norms of collegiality and experimentation: Workplace conditions of school success. *American Educational Research Journal* 19 (3): 325–40.

McLaughlin, M., and J. Talbert. 1993. *Contexts that matter for teaching and learning: Strategic opportunities for meeting the nation's educational goals*. Stanford, CA: Stanford University, Center for Research on the Context of Secondary School Teaching.

———. 2006. *Building school-based teacher learning communities: Professional strategies to improve student achievement*. New York: Teachers College Press.

Mohr, N. No date. Descriptive consultancy. www.nsrfharmony.org/protocol/a_z.html (accessed November 14, 2008).

Newmann, F. 1994. School-wide professional community. *Issues in Restructuring Schools* 6:1–2.

Sternberg, R., and E. Gigorenko. 2000. Triarchic intelligence theory self-assessment. www.docstoc.com/docs/2215602/Triarchic-Theory-of-Intelligences---Robert-Sternberg (accessed June 2, 2009).

Teacher Development Group. 2002. Data driven dialogue. www.nsrfharmony.org/protocol/a_z.html (accessed November 14, 2008).

Wheelan, S., and J. Kesselring. 2005. Link between faculty group development and elementary student performance on standardized tests. *Journal of Educational Research* 98 (6): 323–30, 384.

Yendol-Hoppey, D., and N. Dana. 2009. Commingling action research and PLCs: An illustration of key components. In *ATE Yearbook XVII: Teacher Learning in Small Group Settings*, ed. C. J. Craig and L. F. Deretchin, 54–65). Lanham, MD: Rowman & Littlefield.

Appendix A: Flowchart for Protocol Decision Making

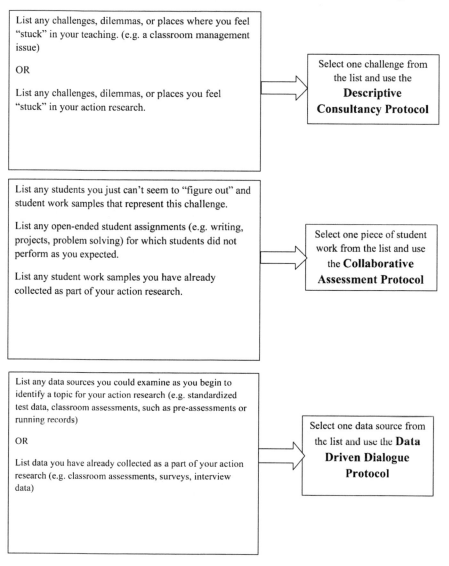

List any challenges, dilemmas, or places where you feel "stuck" in your teaching. (e.g. a classroom management issue)

OR

List any challenges, dilemmas, or places you feel "stuck" in your action research.

Select one challenge from the list and use the **Descriptive Consultancy Protocol**

List any students you just can't seem to "figure out" and student work samples that represent this challenge.

List any open-ended student assignments (e.g. writing, projects, problem solving) for which students did not perform as you expected.

List any student work samples you have already collected as part of your action research.

Select one piece of student work from the list and use the **Collaborative Assessment Protocol**

List any data sources you could examine as you begin to identify a topic for your action research (e.g. standardized test data, classroom assessments, such as pre-assessments or running records)

OR

List data you have already collected as a part of your action research (e.g. classroom assessments, surveys, interview data)

Select one data source from the list and use the **Data Driven Dialogue Protocol**

CHAPTER EIGHT

Developing an Action Research Communication Plan

Stephen L. Maltese Jr., Frances Bond, and Barbara Bisset

> The first thought that came to my mind when I thought of my action
> research was one of fear. I had no idea of what it meant.
>
> —Stacy, teacher intern, Stevenson University

If you are facing the prospect of developing and implementing an action
research project, you may share Stacy's feelings. In this chapter, you will be
introduced to a holistic model for communicating your action research. This
approach will reduce anxiety by demystifying the components and process of
your action research among all stakeholders and help you develop a plan to
communicate information clearly and accurately. This chapter is meant to
be used by teacher interns, in-service teachers, administrators, and college
and university faculty, whose intention it is to support and deliver effective
action research.

By the time you finish reading and thinking about this chapter, you will
be able to do the following:

- Explain what it means to utilize a holistic approach to communication
- Design an action research communication plan that addresses the
  needs of each stakeholder
- Implement your own action research communication plan as a tool
  that will assist you in completing your action research

Preparing for Communication

In previous chapters, the steps and processes of action research and what it means to be a reflective practitioner have been described. In this chapter, the focus is on how your action research can be communicated concisely to all stakeholders by utilizing a holistic approach to communication.

A Holistic Approach to Communication

The term *holistic* refers to the importance of all aspects of a structure. The term is most often associated with medicine, where the complete system is considered, rather than the dissection and treatment of any one single part without regard to the entire body. A holistic approach to communication for an action research project means that the planning, implementation, and results of the research must be thoroughly and accurately communicated to all stakeholders, to ensure a successful experience. Although communication components may vary depending on the stakeholders involved—that is, the students, school-based personnel, Institution of Higher Education (IHE) personnel, the researchers (educational interns, graduate students, or in-service teachers), and parents and guardians—we have found that action research tends to run smoothly if all stakeholders are informed and willing participants.

Your action research communication plan (ARC) will be developed during the planning stages of your action research—that is, issue identification and action planning, discussed in chapter 1. This process will establish an environment in which planned communication becomes a natural component of your classroom practices.

Concise and Systematic Communication

We have all experienced situations where poor communication has led to misunderstandings. You may have had a student who misinterprets an assignment, a parent who is uncomfortable with educational jargon, a supervising teacher who is hesitant about something new you want to try, or a college supervisor who is not familiar with the culture of your school. In each of these situations, clear and concise communication could have alleviated the anxiety that comes along with misunderstandings or a lack of information.

> As a new teacher, my principal told me that when talking with parents about their child's test scores, behavior, or special interventions, I should be clear and concise and refrain from using educational jargon.
>
> —In-service teacher

In order to help your action research to be successful, you must plan for concise communication with each group of stakeholders. Providing a clear picture of why and how your action research is being done—communicated in ways that are easily understood by each group of stakeholders—is critical to a successful project. This chapter will assist you in doing just that.

Clear and concise communication may differ depending upon the stakeholders with whom you interact. Throughout your teacher preparation experience, you probably spent a great deal of your time in courses and classrooms where educational jargon was the language of choice. Any profession, such as medicine, law, or psychology, has its own language. Why is it that we educators expect our language to be universal? Are you confident that the majority of the parents and guardians of your students have a solid understanding of what you are trying to communicate to them when you use profession-specific language? One part of being concise in your communication means that you "unload" jargon-laden language, so that you can communicate effectively with all stakeholders who might be involved with your action research project.

Stop and Reflect

The initial portion of this chapter has introduced you to the concept of a holistic model for concise communication. In this introduction we did the following:

- Identified possible stakeholders
- Explained the importance of developing a clear and concise communication plan in the action research process

Key Questions for Concise Communication

There are many elements to successful communication. The following three key questions will help you identify the information you need to create your action research communication plan.

Key Question 1: What words will I use that clearly convey what I mean?

There are generally three groups of stakeholders who make up your audience. The first is the educational personnel. If you are a teacher intern in an undergraduate or graduate program, or an in-service teacher implementing action research for the first time, this audience might include your college supervisor or professor, the faculty at your school, your school administrators, and your intern colleagues. You might assume that all of these educators understand the process and language of action research. It is important that your communication plan fosters a common understanding of the action research process among all these groups.

A second targeted group is the parents and guardians. Parents and guardians sometimes feel uncomfortable when teachers are throwing around educational jargon. Prior to communicating with parents and guardians, it is a good idea to unload the educational jargon into language that is universally understood.

The third group is your students. Your communication plan for students should explain the activities in the "action" part of your action research, how they will be involved, and how they will benefit from participating. This aspect of your communication will be addressed later in the chapter.

Let's consider some examples of how you might promote a common understanding of terms for the first two groups, educators and parents and guardians.

Example 1

"What do you mean by action research?"

A "textbook response" for educators might be: "Action research is the process of systematically collecting and analyzing student data to improve instructional practice." (If they are keenly interested in learning more about the process, consider sharing this book with them.)

A response for parents and guardians might be: "Action research is a process that allows teachers to use student test results and class work to determine what students are learning and how teachers can best meet their needs."

Example 2

"Can you explain the difference between a formative and summative assessment?"

A textbook response for educators might be: "A formative assessment is an ongoing evaluation process that occurs before completion of an instructional activity and is normally used to plan and modify instruction during the course of learning. A summative assessment is an evaluation carried out at the end of a time period and is intended to document a learner's progress or a program's accomplishments."

A response to parents and guardians might be: "A formative assessment may be graded class work, homework, or a quiz that helps a teacher determine how well students understand what they are being taught. A summative assessment might be a unit test, chapter test, or project that helps a teacher determine what students have learned regarding a unit or chapter that they have just completed."

Example 3
"What do we mean by data?"

A textbook response for educators might be: "Factual information that is organized so that it can be analyzed to make educational decisions."

A response to parents and guardians might be: "Data is information we use to measure our teaching effectiveness and how well a student is doing. Standardized testing is only one of several ways that a teacher evaluates a student's progress. Teachers also use classroom tests, class work, and homework to determine a student's strengths and weaknesses."

Stop and Reflect

Before continuing, take several minutes to reflect on what you have just read. In the parent response, there has been a meaningful effort to avoid assuming that the parents and guardians are familiar with all of the vocabulary that is used in education. This is not to say that parents and guardians are unfamiliar with such terms; however, nothing should be taken for granted. As parents and guardians become more familiar with the educational process and comfortable with the language that is being used in communicating with them, their level of participation may increase.

Collaborative Activity

Using figure 8.1, make a list of the action research words that you will need to define in parent-friendly terms. You might consider pairing up with a colleague and exploring ways to define these words for parents and guardians.

Figure 8.1. Unloading Language

Educational jargon	Universal language

Key Question 2: What questions might school faculty and parents and guardians ask that I must be prepared to answer?

You may be working with a faculty or parents and guardians who are not familiar with or have never heard of action research. If that is the case, it will be essential that you include in your communication plan strategies for informing them about the components and purpose of action research. Faculty and parents and guardians will have different interests or concerns about your project, so you must be prepared with information to answer a variety of questions. In the first chapter of this text, you were introduced to the components of action research. Use chapter 1, along with the questions below, as you prepare to disseminate information to your stakeholders. As you work through these questions, write the answers down in a journal so that you can refer to it when developing your communication plan.

Questions that your faculty might ask could include the following:

- How will I be involved with the intern's action research?
- What is the difference between action research and other forms of research?
- Why conduct action research?
- What is the role of the university in action research?
- Does action research take away from other instructional time?

Prior to presenting your action research ideas to your faculty, it is important that you sit down and discuss these questions with your supervising teacher and university supervisor so nothing comes as a surprise.

Some sample questions from parents or guardians might include the following:

- Why was my child selected for this program?
- What will my child be doing?
- Will this affect my child's grade?
- Will this program take away from the regular classroom instruction or specials?
- Will I be involved in this program?

Communicating with parents and guardians will bring different challenges. Their questions related to action research will likely be centered on the involvement of their children. You must be careful to use appropriate terminology and avoid educational jargon, as discussed above, in responding to their questions. Answers to these questions will vary depending on the specific situation in your school. However, you should be prepared with responses that include the data by which students were selected, the purpose of your action research related to student achievement, information about how your action research will be conducted, and how you expect parents and guardians to be involved.

If you are a classroom teacher, you might consider discussing the answer to this question with your school administrations. If you are a teacher intern, you will want to discuss the answers to these questions with your university supervisor, school supervisor, professors, and possibly the school administration, prior to communicating with parents and guardians, so that you are sure you are following school policy and supporting the educational goals of the school.

Stop and Reflect

In this section, we presented several questions that might be asked by the school faculty and parents and guardians about your action research project. After talking with your college supervisor, what additional questions should you consider? Compile a list of key words or phrases that you would use with parents and guardians or school faculty to answer the potential questions that each of these stakeholders might ask.

Key Question 3: How will I communicate information with my university supervisor, my mentor teacher, college professor (for teacher interns), the administration and faculty at school, and the parents and guardians?

As you begin thinking about the design of your communication plan, you will want to consider three methods of communication: oral, written, and electronic. All three methods present opportunities to define action research for the stakeholders, and help them understand their role in the process.

Communicating with Your University Supervisor
If you are a teacher intern or graduate student, the first step in your action research should be to set up a meeting with your university supervisor or professor. This meeting is simply a discussion. However, planning for this type of oral communication will help you start an important dialogue regarding your action research. It is important that you clearly understand the expectations for your action research, and have an opportunity to ask questions and clarify your understanding. You should discuss the timeline for your action research, the format for documenting the project, and the resources and supports that you can expect while completing the project. Make sure that you take careful notes at this meeting so that you have a reliable record of what you are expected to do.

For each phase of your action research, think about ways you can communicate in writing with your stakeholders. Be sure that you understand the written format that your university supervisor or professor will require you to use to outline your project proposal and document your work, and then carefully follow that format. Maintain careful records of your data collection and keep a log of each activity in your action research. This information will enable you to document your action research in a complete and comprehensive manner.

Electronic communication methods provide several ways to maintain contact with educators and parents and guardians. You can keep your university supervisor informed about your action research through e-mail. You may want to print out your e-mail communications for future reference.

Communicating with Your Mentor Teacher

If you are a teacher intern or have a mentor, you should meet with your mentor to review the university's expectations. Again, this meeting is simply a discussion to ensure that you are on the same page. You will want to review the details of your action research and discuss possible topics for investigation, identify possible target groups of students, or examine available data in order to determine the focus of your action research. During this meeting, be sure to share the notes from the meeting with your university supervisor.

Next, you will want to design and implement a schedule of meetings that provide the two of you with opportunities to review the ongoing development of your action research. Another result of the review may be a meeting with your teaching team to share the goals of your action research and to invite them to contribute to the process. It is important to remember that many of the students who participate in your action research may work with the other members of your teaching team and that those teachers may possess valuable insights regarding those students.

Communicating with School Administration and Faculty

The school administration will want to know the details of your proposed action research, including how students will be involved, and what school resources will be needed to support your research.

Information that you need to convey to the school administrator includes how you will identify the students to be involved in the action research, and the faculty members who will be involved in the project. You should be able to clearly describe the action research proposal, including your issue identification, data collection, and action plan, and how all stakeholders will be informed about the project. You should present a plan to your school administrator and seek information from him or her about how parents, guardians, and faculty should be kept informed about the progress of the project and how the final results should be conveyed.

Ask your school administration if you can present your action research proposal to the school faculty, perhaps through a short presentation at a faculty meeting. Through this presentation, you can keep everyone informed of your work, promote a spirit of collegiality and collaboration among the school faculty, and answer any questions from the audience.

Communicating with Parents and Guardians

Once your action research project plan is complete and the students have been identified, you might want to meet with their parents and guardians to provide an orientation to the project. Be sure to seek guidance from your mentor and school administration on how best to do this. While they don't need to know all the details of your action research, parents and guardians should be informed of the activities in which their child will be engaged. At this meeting, you can explain the project to the parents and guardians (Remember: don't use educational jargon!) and enlist their support for their child's participation. If there is a role for parents and guardians in the program, provide specific details about what you expect parents and guardians to do as they work with their child. As the action research project unfolds, you might want to maintain contact with the parents and guardians, and you may also need to meet with some individually to provide specific information about their child's participation and progress.

There are several written communication methods through which you can maintain contact with parents and guardians. If your school has a newsletter, you could ask to include a short explanation of action research and how it supports the goals of the school, particularly as it relates to student achievement. A letter to the parents and guardians of the identified students in your action research should outline the benefits of the program and how they can support their child's participation. This letter should provide a place for the parents and guardians to sign, giving permission for their child to participate in the program, and contact information should they want to contact you or your mentor teacher during the course of the program. If your action research occurs over several weeks, you may want to send periodic updates to parents and guardians, perhaps in the form of a separate project newsletter.

If the parents and guardians of your students have computers, you may also use e-mail to keep them informed, but be sure to provide alternative means of communication for those who are not electronically connected. If your school has a website, you may ask the school administration for permission to post information about your project. Be sure to follow the rules for student confidentiality on the Internet, as you would for all other forms of communication.

You might want to explore other electronic means of communication such as digital photography. Letting parents and guardians see their child in action is always a great way to encourage support for your project. Remember, however, to always get permission through the proper channels when you are using electronic media. It is essential that all written and electronic communication about your action research be reviewed and approved by your mentor teacher, your university supervisor, and the school administration prior to its distribution. Once your project is complete, you will want to provide summary student achievement information to the parents and guardians and the school administration documenting your action research.

Stop and Reflect

In this section of the chapter, we presented types of communication that should be included in your communication plan. Before completing the collaborative activity, think about the types of communication that you will use with each stakeholder.

Collaborative Activity

With your mentor teacher or another peer, use the collaborative activity chart in figure 8.2, to list the strategies that you will use to communicate with each of your stakeholders.

Figure 8.2.   Collaborative Activity Chart

University supervisor	Mentor teacher	School administration and faculty	Parents

A Model Action Research Communication Plan

To get you started, we are going to provide an example of how an action research communication plan (ARC) evolved and was implemented to facilitate an action research project for an after-school tutorial program called *AfterMath*. Later in this chapter you will be guided through the process of developing your own communication plan based on this model.

Creating an ARC

Beginning in the third week of August, when schools are gearing up for their coming academic year, five university teacher candidates began their year-long internship at an elementary school located in the northern part of Baltimore County, Maryland. One of the requirements of the internship was to conduct an action research project that was directly related to the school improvement plan. Each of the five interns was given the task of designing and implementing an action research project. Three of the interns chose to collaboratively design an after-school tutorial program called *AfterMath*.

The *AfterMath* project incorporated a planned system of concise communication to inform the stakeholders about the inclusion of action research into the after-school tutorial program. The following is a description of how this communication plan unfolded, utilizing a six-step approach.

The Six-Step ARC Planning Process

- Step 1 Getting started
- Step 2 Communicating with your mentor teacher and faculty
- Step 3 Communicating with school-based administrators
- Step 4 Involving the parents and guardians
- Step 5 Engaging the students
- Step 6 Wrapping it up

Step 1: Getting Started

Five education interns from Sparks Elementary School selected math achievement as the focus of their action research project. Throughout their senior year internship, the education interns at Stevenson University participated in a seminar class. One focus of the seminar was to introduce action research, ensure that the interns thoroughly understood the process, and provide assistance in the formulation and implementation of an action research project at their placement professional development school (PDS). A university PDS supervisor conducted related discussion sessions at the corresponding PDS partner school. This ongoing opportunity for discussion and collaboration throughout the school year was invaluable as the interns learned about the components of action research, examined school data to determine student needs, and began formulating their action plans.

Initially in step 1, only two of the stakeholder groups were involved, the interns and the university faculty. Step 1 served as a vehicle to introduce the interns to the components of action research. As they developed a communication plan at Sparks Elementary School, they applied what they learned to clearly identify their issue to investigate, create an action plan, and then determine how they would present it to their other stakeholders.

Step 2: Communicating with Your Mentor Teacher and Faculty

The interns at Sparks Elementary School added a stakeholder group. The mentor teachers became involved in the formation of the action research project. The college supervisor/intern/mentor teacher conference became an important communication format in this step. These conferences ensured that all those involved in the action research process had a common understanding of terminology, components, and stakeholder roles.

Step 3: Communicating with School-Based Administrators

The audience at Sparks Elementary School was further expanded by including the school-based administrators in the action research process. This inclusion served to expand the support that the school could provide for the action research projects as the administration learned about the action research model and how it could be implemented at the elementary school.

Prior to the inclusion of the school-based administrators, the interns, in conjunction with their mentor teachers, prepared a rationale for the topic of their action research. In preparing their rationales, they included descriptions and vocabulary that reflected their review of literature and best practices. The stakeholders, who were previously involved in steps 1 and 2, continued to be engaged in the process. The stakeholders worked collaboratively to contribute resources, guidance, and professional expertise to the interns as they were formulating their action research projects.

Step 4: Involving the Parents and Guardians

The parents and guardians were the next group of stakeholders to be addressed in the plan. Prior to contacting the parents and guardians, the interns needed to assemble the contact information related to each student. This step is critical and needs to be thoroughly researched.

It's important to remember that education exists in a world populated with nuclear and blended families, guardianships, children being raised by grandparents, and single parents. The interns were aware that the first impression they made could be critical to student participation and at-home support. To provide them with accurate information, the interns met with the administration and support staff, classroom teachers, the school nurse, and the guidance counselor. As the contact information was being collected, the interns drafted a letter that defined the purpose of the program, the specific curriculum objectives, the program schedule, intern contact information, and a permission form. After the permission forms were returned, the interns and their mentor teachers scheduled a meeting with all of the contacted parents and guardians. During this meeting, the objective of the program was revisited, the materials were previewed, and a question-and-answer session was conducted.

The ongoing school/home communication plan, utilizing oral, written, and electronic communication, was detailed. All of what has been included in this chapter has emphasized the importance of the interdependence of the stakeholders. This step embodies that principle.

Step 5: Engaging the Students

The interns again expanded the stakeholder group, this time to include the students who would be invited to participate. Step 5 was developed and implemented in conjunction with step 4 (parent and guardian information). As the interns finalized their preparations to contact the parents and guardians, they prepared a presentation for the students who were selected to participate in the program. The student presentation was scheduled to coincide with the distribution of the parent letter that students received at the end of the presentation.

The interns invited all of the students from the different classes to the school library to explain the *AfterMath* program. The presentation was designed to inform the students as to why they had been selected, the types of activities and incentives that would be included in the program, the program schedule, and the importance of sharing the letter with their parents or guardians. Upon the return of the permission forms, the interns commenced their action research.

Step 6: Wrapping It Up

The objective of the interns was to plan and implement a successful strategy to conclude or wrap up their action research. The interns had started planning for this step during their formal introduction to action research in step 1. As they drafted their proposals, the interns were required to develop a system of data collection that would assist them in analyzing data, identifying connections to their teaching, reflecting on their experiences, and compiling a report on their action research projects. This ongoing process began with the start of the *AfterMath* program.

As a result of conferencing with their mentor teachers and college supervisor, the interns decided to use a daily journal to document each session's objective and formative assessment, the resources used to teach the session, and student work samples. The interns also used the journal to reflect on the experience and consider the connections to their teaching. The comprehensive nature of the journal allowed interns to quickly access information that they used as they prepared for the conclusion of the *AfterMath* program.

The conclusion of the program was divided into two parts: the completion of the *AfterMath* student program and drafting a report that summarized each intern's action research. The final session of *AfterMath* was devoted to disseminating information to the parents and guardians of the participating students and celebrating their accomplishments. The drafting of the final report was easy because, along with the quantitative data collected regularly, the daily journaling completed by each intern provided a wealth of information.

Stop and Reflect

When you reflect on what you have just read, you can identify many of the components that comprise an action research communication plan (ARC). ARC's genesis began with the people it served, the stakeholders. The more stakeholders are engaged in the process, the greater the possibility that the action research project will be successfully implemented.

Each of the six steps that is described and modeled is reliant on previous steps that occurred in the development of the communication plan. This interdependence clearly demonstrates the holistic nature of the communication plan.

Developing Your Action Research Communication Plan

As you read about the implementation of the *AfterMath* project, you were introduced to the specific steps that were followed to develop and implement a communication plan. Let's review the steps:

- Step 1: Getting started
- Step 2: Communicating with your mentor teacher and faculty
- Step 3: Communicating with school-based administrators
- Step 4: Involving the parents and guardians
- Step 5: Engaging the students
- Step 6: Wrapping it up

As you think about implementing your own communication plan, complete the following chart in each section. When you are finished, you will have your own clear and concise action research communication plan. As you move through each step, be sure to consider:

- How stakeholders can be brought into the process

- How information can be synthesized from educational literature and best practices to present a clear plan for the action research
- The types of communication employed to convey the information

As was mentioned previously, you may not have the same resources that were available to the interns at Sparks Elementary. Not having the same resources will not inhibit your ability to develop your plan. You will simply investigate what resources and support are available to you at your college, university, or school system and consider the questions that you will need to ask. As you think about each step, record your ideas in the appropriate chart.

Developing Your Action Research Communication Plan
Step 1: Getting Started

- The graphic organizer in figure 8.3 will help you identify important components for your action research communication plan (ARC). Consider using a personal journal to record your information, or reproduce this graphic organizer in a way that allows you to fit all the information you might need to record.

Look at the information under the Components and Questions columns. The Examples column provides some suggested ideas for you to consider. As you think about each component, complete the Your Plans column of the chart. Use the information you gathered in the previous exercises in this chapter to help you complete the chart.

Stop and Reflect

Review your step 1 chart with your college supervisor, mentor teacher, or team leader to be sure that you are on the right track. Once you and your college supervisor or mentor teacher have conferred, you are ready to complete the rest of your plan.

Step 2 to Step 5:

Now complete the next action research graphic organizer, as shown in figure 8.4. Again, consider using a personal journal to record your information, or reproduce this graphic organizer in a way that allows you to fit all the information you might need to record. As you work through the process, consider the stages of action research that Pelton identified in chapter 1:

1. Issue identification
2. Data collection
3. Action planning
4. Plan activation
5. Outcome assessment

As you reflect upon your own school setting, add additional audiences to your communication plan as needed.

Stop and Reflect

You may already realize that by completing the graphic organizer in figure 8.4, you have successfully moved through steps 2–5 of your communication plan:

Figure 8.3. Graphic organizer: Action research communication plan, step 1.

Components	Questions	Examples	Your plans
Stakeholders	Who will need to be included in your communication plan?	University supervisor, mentor teacher, school administration, faculty, parents, students	
Information	What concepts and ideas do your stakeholders need to understand and be able to apply?	An understanding of the process of action research An understanding of their role in the process An understanding of the value of action research to the students	
Information resources	What print, nonprint, and electronic materials will you need to communicate the details of your action research?	Review the school improvement plan. Review the school achievement data. Conduct a literature review for possible action research topics.	
Communication format	What means of oral, written, and electronic communication are available to you?	Refer to "Collaborative Activity."	
Timeline	What is the timeline for developing your communication plan?	August–September	

- Step 2: Communicating with your mentor teacher and faculty
- Step 3: Communicating with school-based administrators
- Step 4: Involving the parents and guardians
- Step 5: Engaging the students

Step 6: Wrapping It Up

You have implemented your action research project, but there is still one additional step. In step 6, you will reflect on what you accomplished and what impact this project had on the students with whom you worked. You will want to reflect on how your communication plan enhanced the process and kept stakeholders well informed and engaged throughout the project. Use the chart in figure 8.5 to record your reflections and the actions you will take to wrap up your project. Once again, you can use a personal journal to

Figure 8.4. Graphic organizer: Action Research Communication Plan, steps 2–5.

Components	Questions	University supervisor	Mentor	School administration and faculty	Parents	Students
Information	What concepts and ideas does this stakeholder need to understand and be able to apply?					
Information resources	What print, nonprint and electronic materials will you need to communicate the details of your action research?					
Communication format	How will information be communicated to the stakeholder?					
Timeline	What is the timeline for developing your communication plan?					

record your information, or reproduce this graphic organizer in a way that allows you to fit all the information you might need to record.

It is strongly suggested that you implement the steps as they are numbered. However, be aware that many of these steps may overlap. As you implement the steps, you may discover that your specific school environment and the associated stakeholders may require you to modify the steps. The important thing to remember is that you have a plan of communication that seeks out the stakeholders and addresses the needs of the specific groups.

Stop and Reflect

After reviewing and reflecting on the data generated by your action research, what modifications would you consider making to your communication plan to ensure that all stakeholders understand and benefit from the project?

Closing Reflections

A well-designed and thoroughly implemented communication plan will involve all stakeholders in the process and will support the successful implementation of your action research project. Your communication plan addresses these essential elements of a holistic model of action research communication:

- It provides clarity for the intern about the requirements of the project.

Figure 8.5. Graphic Organizer: Action Research Communication Plan, Step 6.

Components	Questions	Your plan
Stakeholders	How did you involve each group?	
Information	In what ways were your stakeholders well informed throughout the process?	
Information resources	What print, nonprint, and electronic materials were most effective in communicating your message?	
Communication format	Which strategies/methods were most effective in communicating your message to the various stakeholders?	
Timeline	Was your original timeline realistic? If not, how might you have modified it?	

- It provides opportunities for all stakeholders to understand action research and their involvement in the process. The plan clearly defines the role for each stakeholder, identifies the needed information and resources to be communicated, and establishes a timeline for the completion of all aspects of action research.
- It promotes collegiality among the interns, university personnel, and the school staff. Each stakeholder is respected and his or her participation in the action research process is seen as important to its success.
- It promotes student achievement through including parents and guardians in the process and clearly identifying how they can support their child's work.

In the beginning of this chapter, you read a quote from Stacey, a Sparks Elementary School intern, as she described her feelings and fears about tackling an action research project. As Sparks Elementary implemented a holistic model of action research communication, and implemented a clear and consistent plan for communicating about action research (the ARC), Stacey had the opportunity to learn how such a plan helped her effectively conduct her action research. At the conclusion of the *AfterMath* program, Stacey reflected upon her experience:

> When I was initially introduced to the concept of developing and conducting an action research project, I was very overwhelmed. There were many guidelines to follow concerning researching best practices, collecting data, and analyzing results. I honestly did not know where to begin. I was very worried about organizing my ideas and information in a professional manner. I was also nervous about attempting to appropriately explain my thoughts to my senior seminar instructors, as well as my school and college supervisors. Fortunately, I was able to build a meaningful dialogue with my instructors and supervisors, helping me establish an ongoing system of communication with them. In turn, I was able to use both verbal and electronic modes of communication to share results and receive feedback. Without such communication, I would not have been able to conduct my action research plan effectively.

Learning to communicate concisely and clearly with all of your partners in the educational community is a skill that will benefit you both now and throughout your entire teaching career.

Questions for Review and Reflection

1. Define the holistic approach to communication when incorporated into an action research proposal.

2. Identify the steps you would follow to design an action research communication plan that addresses the needs of each stakeholder.
3. Design a schedule for implementing the steps of your action research communication plan.

Index

action planning: beneficiaries of, 45; collaboration during, 9; conversation formats supporting, 123–24, *139*; process of, 6

action research: best practices in, 2; collaboration in, 9–10, 141–59; communicating, 161; communication plan as developed, 161–80; communication plan steps of development, 171–72, 175, *176–77*; community, 142–43; context's importance in, 13–42; conversation model for, *118*; credibility of, 13, 15; data collection before, 32; data in process of, 154; developing mindset of, 2–3; early research on perspective of, 87–88; examples of, 131–32; feelings about, 179; focus, 43, *51*, 51–52; framing, 43–66; impetus for, 148; interaction analysis as tool for, 93–94; interventions designed with, 133–34; issue identification as starting point for, 4; key strategies of, 1–11; learning from student work during, 150–54, *152*; microteaching as tool for, 91–92; mindset, 1–3, 4; as mindset toward teaching, 1; oral inquiry as supporting steps of, 117–40; oral inquiry template, *138*; outcome assessment in, 7; perspective, 84–85; placement school of, 19–20; plan activation stage of, 7; as problem solving, 148–49; process, 5; protocols supporting, *148*, 148–57; reasons for conducting, 130; school's improvement plan and, 56; self-study as tool for, 92–93; student characteristics in, 13; study as framed, 43–66; teaching strategies and, 64; tools for collaboration in, 141–59; topic, 43; utilizing process in, 2–7, 4–6; video studies from improving classroom teaching-learning performances, 83–113; wrapping up, 173–74. *See also* action planning

181

activation. *See* plan activation
administration, communication with
    school, 168–69, 172
AfterMath, 170; conclusion of, 174
Agnes Russell Elementary School, 91
analysis: data, 154–57, *155*; mirrors
    for, 98; through video, 83. *See
    also* interaction analysis; outcome
    analysis
Anderson, William G., 89; self-study
    and, 92
anxiety, 162
approaches: to communication as
    holistic, 161–62; of Mixed Methods
    research, 69, 80–81; philosophical
    difference between quantitative and
    qualitative, 70–71
assessment: collaborative, 150–54,
    152, *154*; conversations, 129–31;
    designing process of, 130; forms
    of, 54–55; mirrors for, 98. *See also*
    outcome assessment
attention: desire for, 150; given to data,
    8–9

baseline information, on student
    performance, 47
behaviors: conferencing, 100; interactive,
    89; as learning outcome, 56
Bellack, Arno, 88, 89
benefits: of collaboration, 142; of
    understanding context, 15; of video,
    104
brainstorming, 126, 156

change: being flexible to, 7–8; as
    implemented in teaching, 63; in
    interactions, 96; in student learning,
    45, 48–49
characteristics. *See* student
    characteristics
checklists. *See* observational checklists
class rankings, 72

classroom: instruction, 95, *110*;
    management, *109*; physical features
    of, 26–27, *27*; research, 87; rubrics
    for assessing performance in, 101;
    social climate of, 95, *109*; teaching-
    learning performances as improved,
    83–113
coaching, conversations, 129–30
Coalition for Essential Schools, 146
collaboration, 2; in action research,
    9–10, 141–59; for action researchers,
    9–10; activity for, 165–66, 170;
    benefits of, 142; between school
    faculty, 157; structured conversational
    protocols role in, 142; thought
    clarified through, 9; tools for, 141–59
collection. *See* data collection
communication: action research plan of,
    161–80; action research supported
    by, 117; concise and systematic,
    162–63, 179; developing action
    research plan of, 161–80; electronic,
    168; holistic approach to, 161–62;
    key questions for concise, 163–65;
    with mentor teacher, 168, 172;
    methods of, 167; model plan for,
    170–71; with parents/guardians,
    164–66, 169, 172–73; photography
    in, 169–70; poor, 162; preparing for,
    162; with school administration,
    168–69, 172; with stakeholders, 163;
    with university supervisor, 167–68;
    unloading language for, *165*; words
    used for, 163; in writing, 167, 169.
    See also oral inquiry
community: building conversations,
    125–26; characteristics, 18; data
    collection on, 27–28; developing
    action research, 142–43;
    expectations about, 28; extended,
    28, *29*, *30*; factors in learning
    environment, 14; formulating, 143;
    norms as established, 143–44

concept maps, 59
confidence, 122
confidentiality, in data collection, 23
consent: informed, 39; written, 39
context: in action research as important,
    13–42; benefits of understanding, 15;
    collecting data on factors of, 19–23,
    19–28, 25, 27–28; describing details
    of, 13; instructional implications of
    factors of, 28–30, 29–30. See also
    school context
contextual factors, 19–23, 19–28, 25,
    27–28
conversation(s): action planning
    supported by formats of, 123–
    24, 139; assessment, 129–31;
    benchmarking, 127–28; check for
    understanding types of, 130–31;
    coaching, 129–30; community-
    building, 125–26; cumulative, 124,
    126; data collection supporting
    formats of, 123, 126, 139; for
    decision making, 121; design, 117;
    disposition created through, 135;
    for exchanging knowledge, 121–22;
    expectations cleared through, 139;
    exploratory, 125; formats, 123–31;
    forum established by, 117; framework
    for thinking about, 119; goal-setting,
    128–29; inferential, 124; insight
    from, 129; issue identification
    supported by, 120; learning, 117–40;
    model for action research, 118; as
    natural, 135; networks built through,
    134–35; outcome assessment
    supporting, 127, 130–31; plan
    activation supported by, 123–24,
    133; planning of, 120, 123; planning
    supported by, 126; purpose, 120;
    strategies, 118; among teachers, 132–
    33; template of oral inquiry learning,
    136; thinking focused through, 122;
    as tools, 117; topics for, 121; types

as defined, 127; for understanding,
    122–23. See also oral inquiry
creative thinking, 156
credibility, of action research, 13, 15
culture, 10

data: in action research process, 154;
    analysis, 154–57, 155; attention
    given to, 8–9; on community,
    27–28; confidentiality in collection
    of, 23; descriptive observational
    systems, 88; documenting sources
    of, 18–19; driven dialogue protocol,
    154–57, 155, 159; forms of,
    72–73; locating sources of, 16–18;
    from Mixed Methods design, 69;
    primary sources of, 17; secondary
    sources of, 18; sensitive, 22–23;
    sources, 16–19, 41, 52; sources
    for answering research questions,
    52, 53; surprised by, 157; survey,
    156; tables, 34; teacher journal as
    source of, 53; triangulating, 80;
    using, 2; using resources for, 17–18;
    value of collecting, 31–32; written
    consent for collecting, 39. See also
    data collection; qualitative data;
    quantitative data
databases, research, 10
data collection, 6; before action
    research, 32; on community, 27–28;
    confidentiality in, 23; on contextual
    factors, 19–23, 19–28, 25, 27–28;
    conversation formats supporting, 123,
    126, 139; levels of, 14; process, 14–15
decisions: conversations for making,
    121; making for protocols, 159
demographics, student, 72–73
design: conversation, 117; examples of
    Mixed Methods research, 73, 75–80;
    of interventions, 133–34; Mixed
    Methods research, 67–81; research,
    67–81

desire: for attention, 150; for learning
outcomes, 93, 98, 104; for student
learning changes, 45, 48–49

education: descriptive observational
systems in, 89; research, 90; teacher,
88–89, 181n1; through teaching,
86. *See also* learning; special
education
effectiveness: evaluating teachers', 2;
teaching, 94; teaching strategies,
64–65
elementary grades, framing issues, 55–56
environment. *See* learning environment
ethnicity, 24
examples: of action research, 131–32; of
Mixed Methods research design, 73,
75–80
expectations: clearing, *139*; about
community, 28; norms defining,
143–44
experiences: of presenter during
protocol, 147; shared, 126
experts, consulting with, 9

facilities, school, 25–26
factors. *See* contextual factors
feedback, 1; corrective, *112*; tools, 89;
video used for, 84
feelings, about action research, 179
FIAC. *See* Flanders Interaction Analysis
Categories
Flanders, Ned, 88, 93
Flanders Interaction Analysis
Categories (FIAC), 93, 99, *112*
flexibility, 7–8
focus: action research, 43, *51*, 51–52;
areas for video projects, 96; from
conversations, 122; establishing, 119–
20; of meetings, 145; research, 52
forms: of assessment, 54–55; of data,
72–73
forum, 117

gender, 72
goals, 127; conversations for setting,
128–29; identifying achievable, 128
guardians. *See* parents

ideas, student, *112*
identification. *See* issue identification
inquiry. *See* oral inquiry
insight, from conversations, 129
instruction: classroom, 95, *110*;
differentiating, 10; factors impacting,
30–31, *31*
interaction: behaviors of, 89; group,
145; monitoring changes in, 96
interaction analysis, 83, 85, 90; as
action research tool, 93–94; strategy
of, 93–94
interventions: action research used for
developing, 133–34; design of, 133–34
intuitions, teacher, 5
issue identification, 155; action research
focus as starting point in, 43; as
action research starting point, 4;
conversation purpose established for
supporting, 120
issues: common framing, 62–63; early
childhood framing, 55; elementary
grades framing, 55–56; middle grades
framing, 57, 59, *59*; secondary grades
framing, 59–61, *61*; special education
framing, 61–62, *62*

Jackson, Philip, 86
journal. *See* teacher journal
Joyce, Bruce, 89; microteaching as used
by, 91

knowledge: conversations for
exchanging, 121–22; reality of,
70–72

learning: action research video studies
and, 83–113; conditions of, 13;

conversations, 117–40; desired
changes in student, 45, 48–49;
enriching, 1; feedback/information
on students', 1; performance domains
of teaching and, 95; relationship
between teaching and, 84–85;
teaching as helping student, 49–50;
about teaching while teaching,
10–11; theory of social, 119. *See also*
problem-based learning
learning environment, 8, 10; community
factors in, 14; impacts on, 14
learning outcomes, 54; addressing, 60;
behavior as, 56; desired, 93, 98, 104;
identifying, 43, 45; skills developed
by, 60; specifying, 49; term as used,
48
levels, of data collection, 14
librarians, 10
Life in Classrooms (Jackson), 86

meetings, focus of, 145
mentors, 9; communication with, 168,
172
methods: of communication, 167. *See
also* Mixed Methods research
microteaching, 90; as action research
tool, 91–92; strategy of, 91; video
strategy of, 83, 85
middle grades: action research across,
57; framing issues, 57, 59, 59
mindset, action research, 1–3, 4
Mixed Methods research: design,
67–81; either-or v., 60–70; examples
of designs of, 73, 75–80; practical
approach of, 80–81; quantitative/
qualitative variables interconnected
in, 68; reason for, 68–69; selection
of, 68; triangulating data within
design of, 80; value of approach, 69

National Board for Professional
Teaching Standards, 101

National Center for Education Statistics
(NCES), 18
National School Reform Faculty, 146
NCES. *See* National Center for
Education Statistics
networks, 134–35
newsletters, 169
No Child Left Behind Act (2001), 24
norms, 143–44

observational checklists, *112*
observational systems: descriptive,
88–89, 98, 100; development/use of
descriptive, 88–89; video study's use
of descriptive, 98–99
optimism, 133
oral inquiry: action research steps
supported by, 117–40; as conversation
model for action research, *118*;
through learning conversations, 136–
37; learning conversation template,
136; process of, 136; template of
action research, *138*
outcome analysis, 154
outcome assessment: in action research,
7; conversation formats supporting,
127, 130–31

parents: communication with,
164–66, 169, 172–73; guidance for
communication with, 169
PATHWISE, 101
performance(s): assessing, 101; in
classroom, 101; domains of teaching
and learning, 95; teaching-learning,
83–113
Performance Assessment for California
Teachers, 101
photography, 169–70
plan activation, conversation formats
supporting, 123–24, 133
planning: conversation formats supporting,
126. *See also* action planning

plans. *See* action planning; school
    improvement plan
praise, 99, *112*
principals, conferencing behaviors of
    teachers and, 100
problem-based learning (PBL), 59
process: of action planning, 6; of
    action research, 2–7, *4–6*, 154; of
    assessment, 130; communication
    plan, 178; data collection, 14–15;
    of oral inquiry, 136; research, 9; as
    utilized in action research, 2–7, *4–6*
Project Zero, 146
protocols, 141; action research
    supporting, *148*, 148–57;
    collaborative assessment, 150–54,
    152, *154*, *159*; common features of,
    146; data-driven dialogue, 154–57,
    155, *159*; debriefing during end
    of, 147; decision making, *159*;
    descriptive consultancy, 148–48,
    149, *159*; development of, 146;
    group interaction and, 145; presenter
    as observer during, 146; presenter
    as personal experience during, 147;
    roles taken during, 146; structured
    conversational, 142; success of, 153;
    as tools for focusing meetings, 145;
    virtual, 145

qualitative data: in Mixed Methods
    approach, 68; quantitative data v.,
    70; sources for conducting research
    with, 73, *74–75*; sources of, 73,
    74–75
quality, of teachers, 94–95
quantitative data: incomplete story
    told by, 68; in Mixed Methods
    approach, 68; qualitative data v., 70;
    techniques for collecting, 73; tips for
    working with, 72–73
questions: bringing research focus
    into research, 52; early childhood

framing, 56; instructional, 97;
    probing, 126; research, 45–47, 53;
    strategic use of, 129. *See also* oral
    inquiry

reality, nature of, 70–72
reasons: for conducting action research,
    130; for Mixed Methods research,
    68–69
reflection: in action, 3, 9–10, 141, 143;
    in action research communication
    plan, 177–78; mirrors for, 98; by
    teachers on actions, 3
research: classroom, 87; databases,
    10; design, 67–81; education, 90;
    focus, 52; librarians and, 10; process,
    9; qualitative v. quantitative, 67;
    questions, 45–47, 52–53; video
    technology in, 89. *See also* action
    research
resources: for data, 17–18; school,
    25–26
response to intervention (RtI), 56
RtI. *See* response to intervention
rubrics: for assessing classroom
    performance, 101; video and, 101

school context: data collection in,
    14–15; data collection on factors of,
    19–23, 19–28, *25*, *27–28*
school improvement plan, 56
schools: facilities, 25–26; resources,
    25–26
school system, placement school v.,
    19–20, *20–21*, *23–24*, *35–39*
scores. *See* test scores
secondary grades, framing issues, 59–61,
    61
Seidel, Steve, 151
self-study, 90; as action research tool,
    92–93; clinical tasks in, 93; twelve
    steps of, 92–93; video strategy of,
    83, 85

setting, goals, 128–29
socioeconomic status, 24, 72
sources: for answering data research
 questions, 52, 53; data, 16–19,
 41, 52; documenting data, 18–19;
 locating data, 16–18; primary data,
 17; secondary data, 18; using data,
 17–18
special education: framing issues, 61–62,
 62; teachers, 61–62
stakeholders: action research
 communication plan addressing
 needs of, 161; in communication
 plan process, 178; communication
 with, 163
standards: meeting, 1. See also state
 standards
state standards, 49, 57
strategies: of action research, 1–11;
 conversation, 118; of interaction
 analysis, 93–94; of microteaching,
 83, 85, 91; self-study, 83, 85; video,
 83, 85. See also teaching strategies
student(s): demographics, 72–73;
 desired changes in learning of, 45,
 48–49; engagement, 95, 111, 173;
 feedback/information on learning
 by, 1; ideas of, 112; needs of, 43;
 number in study of, 62–63; progress,
 63; teaching as helping learning by,
 49–50; tracking scores of, 150–51;
 work, 150–54, 152. See also student
 work
student characteristics: in action
 research study, 13; data on, 72–73
student work, 150–54, 152
studies, action research video, 83–113
study(ies): framing, 43–66; length of,
 63–64; number of students in, 62–63
study rationale, 45
success, of protocols, 153
systems. See observational systems;
 school system

teacher journal, 3; as data source, 53;
 observations recorded in, 53
teachers: action oriented, 1;
 communication with mentor, 168,
 172; conferencing behaviors of
 principals and, 100; conversations
 among, 132–33; effective, 109;
 evaluation of effectiveness of, 2;
 expertise of, 1; intuitions of, 5;
 mentor, 9; praise by, 99; preparation,
 90; quality of, 94–95; reflection on
 actions by, 3; responsive, 2, 10–11;
 special education, 61–62; video in
 education of, 89–90
teaching: action research as mindset
 toward, 1; action research video
 studies and, 83–113; as complex,
 142; early research on study of,
 87; effectiveness, 94; good traits
 of, 87; history of study of, 84,
 86–88; implementing changes
 in, 63; improving, 86; learning
 about teaching while, 10–11;
 performance domains of learning
 and, 95; relationship between
 learning and, 84–85; research-
 based effective guides of action for,
 109; student learning as helped
 by, 49–50; in teacher preparation
 program, 143
teaching strategies: action research for
 documenting use of, 64; as content-
 specific, 59; effectiveness of, 64–65;
 multiple, 54–55
template(s): action research oral
 inquiry, 138; of oral inquiry learning
 conversation, 136
test scores, 1
Third International Mathematics and
 Science Study (TIMSS), 90
tool(s): for action research, 91–94,
 141–49; for collaboration, 141–59;
 conversations as, 117; feedback, 89

topics: choosing action research, 43; for conversation, 121

triangulation, 54; of data sets, 94; of data within Mixed Methods research design, 80

understanding: checking for, 126–27; context, 15; conversations for, 122–23; types of conversations, 130–31

video: analysis through, 83; assessment criteria used for study with, 101; becoming effective with, 94–95; benefits of using, 104; emergence of teaching-learning study through, 89–90; large-scale projects in research, 90; library, 90; performance domains observed using, 95; permanent record provided by, 104; perspectives captured by, 104; pioneers in research/feedback use of, 84; possible focus areas for projects with, 96; in research, 89; rubrics used for study with, 101; strategies, 83, 85; studies for improving classroom teaching-learning performances, 83–113; study's use of descriptive observational category systems, 98; in teacher education, 181n1

The Way Teaching Is (Jackson), 86
work. See student work
writing, communication in, 167, 169

~

About the Contributors

Ellen Ballock, PhD, began her career in education as a second-grade teacher. She has taught in the United States and abroad. She currently works as an assistant professor at Towson University in Maryland, where she lives out her passions for learning through collaboration and action research in her teaching and research.

Sean F. Biancaniello, MEd, graduated with a degree in psychology and completed teaching certification in K–12 mathematics. For the past five years he has taught middle school mathematics in two urban districts serving struggling learners. In each of those years his students have demonstrated success on the state assessment, and he has been invited to share his work on how conversations make a difference with middle school students at several national and state conferences.

Stefan L. Biancaniello, PhD, has forty years of experience in education as a classroom educator, curriculum and assessment director, principal, staff developer, and educational consultant. During that career he has also served ten years as adjunct professor for the Duquesne University Graduate School of Education. He is the coauthor of a chapter in a college textbook on technology and literacy and contributing author on several articles focusing on the impact of technology on literacy learning. He has served as a district fellow to the University of Pittsburgh Learning Research and Development

Center, Institute for Learning and is currently serving on the board of directors for the Pennsylvania Staff Development Council and as a member of the National Staff Development Council Academy.

Barbara Bisset, MS, began her career as an elementary school teacher and subsequently worked with faculty and students as a resource teacher, assistant principal, and principal. She is the former principal of Sparks Elementary School, a Maryland and National Blue Ribbon School, where there is a thriving partnership as a professional development school with Stevenson University. Ms. Bisset is currently the executive director of professional development for the Baltimore County Public Schools system.

Frances Bond, PhD, has been an educator for more than forty years. Her professional career in early childhood education and teacher education at Towson University included teaching graduate and undergraduate courses, chairing the early childhood department, and associate dean in the College of Education. Dr. Bond has also provided education and cross-cultural training to Peace Corps volunteers overseas and served as special assistant to the U.S. Secretary of Education. She has authored articles on teacher education, early childhood curriculum, parenting, and grandparenting.

Linda A. Catelli, PhD, is a professor of education at Dowling College and director of the PDS partnerships. She holds emeritus status at Queens College/CUNY, has a BA from Hunter College, and an MA and EdD from Teachers College, Columbia University. She is the founder of two partnership programs entitled Project SCOPE I and II and was nationally recognized and honored as a pioneer in school-college collaboration by the AAHE in 1990. She received the Faculty Achievement Award from CUNY for creative achievement and pioneering work in partnerships and the Pride Award from Dowling College. She has spoken and published articles, action research papers, chapters, and books on a wide range of topics. She is the coeditor of *Commitment to Excellence: Transforming Teaching and Teacher Education in Inner-City and Urban Settings*, a coauthor of the 2009 book *Analyzing Effective Teaching Performance*, and more recently in 2010 she authored a chapter in the groundbreaking book *Collaboration in Education*.

Rachel Carpenter Heller, BA, is a 2010 graduate of West Virginia University's dual-degree, five-year teacher education program, the Benedum Collaborative. Her teaching certifications are in elementary education and special education.

Stephanie Cucunato, MEd, is completing her seventh year in education serving several school districts as a special education teacher, classroom teacher, and reading specialist. During each of those years her students have demonstrated achievement success on state assessments. She was recognized in 2006 as a Teacher of Excellence and has been invited to present her work on conversations that make a difference for student learning at several national and state conferences.

Reagan Curtis, PhD, is currently associate professor of educational psychology, program evaluation, and research methods in the Department of Technology, Learning, and Culture at West Virginia University. Reagan teaches across the spectrum of research methodologies including statistics, program evaluation, action research, mixed methodologies, and qualitative research. His diverse research interests include the development of mathematical understanding in infancy through elementary school, promotion of equity in STEM (science, technology, engineering, and mathematics) educational and career paths, and exploration of tools and pedagogical approaches to facilitate online instruction at the university level.

Diane Davis, PhD, is currently an associate professor in the School of Education at the College of Notre Dame of Maryland. Prior to coming to the College of Notre Dame of Maryland to serve as the professional development school coordinator, she retired from the Bowie State University as professor in the Department of Education. She also taught in the Baltimore public schools for seven years. She received her PhD from the University of Maryland and has served in various leadership roles including director of student teaching and interim chair of the Department of Education. While coordinator of the professional development schools, she developed a mentoring course and action research course for school-based teachers. She has presented at both the national and state professional development school conferences in the area of action research.

Marjorie Leppo, PhD, is a professor in the Department of Health, Human Performance, and Leisure Studies at Howard Universit,y where she has taught for more than twenty-five years. Dr. Leppo has also taught at the community college level and in grades K–12 in the Baltimore public schools. She received her PhD from the University of Maryland. Dr. Leppo has a broad experience in education administration, as well as teaching. Her current teaching responsibilities include courses in research design, human growth and development, and psychology of sport. She has presented at both the national and state professional development school conferences in the area of action research.

Steve Maltese, MS, began his career in education as an elementary school teacher, eventually moving to teaching middle school mathematics. During this part of his career, he also had an opportunity to teach coursework on alternative forms of energy and energy conservation. Following the conclusion of his middle school teaching, Steve worked as a curriculum developer for a distance learning educational firm and then joined The School of Education at Stevenson University, where he currently serves as an adjunct professor.

David W. Nicholson, PhD, is professor of education at Stevenson University in Maryland. Dr. Nicholson has taught courses in action research at both the undergraduate and graduate levels and coauthored an article on an action research study conducted in a high school English classroom.

Neal Shambaugh, PhD, is an associate professor and graduate program coordinator of instructional design and technology at West Virginia University. His degrees in management science, curriculum and instruction, and instructional systems design are from Virginia Tech. He is the author of two textbooks on instructional design. Since 1999, he has been a university liaison with a public elementary/middle school and has mentored action research with new and experienced teachers.

Jaci Webb-Dempsey, PhD, a former high school art teacher, currently teaches at Fairmont State University, where she coordinates the action research sequence for teacher candidates in the undergraduate and graduate programs and provides supportive professional development for university liaisons and PDS faculty. She has also worked with statewide efforts in West Virginia to promote principal leadership through school-based action research teams and with colleagues at West Virginia University to study the action research process.

~

About the Editor

Dr. Robert P. Pelton is currently a professor in the School of Education at Stevenson University, Stevenson, Maryland. Prior to working at the university level, Robert had an accomplished K–12 teaching career. He began teaching students with exceptional learning needs in an integrated K–third grade classroom, went on to teach middle and high school social studies, then returned to special education where he worked with middle school students categorized as having emotional and behavioral disorders. Through all these experiences, Dr. Pelton saw the value in using classroom based data to shape his instructional methods.

Dr. Pelton has presented nationally and internationally on the topic of action research. Notably, he was invited as a panelist by the International Council on Education for Teaching (ICET) World Assembly in Hong Kong to address the topic of using action research in teacher preparation programs around the world. He is very active in professional development schools, where he assists teacher interns in using classroom data within the action research process to make instructional decisions. Dr. Pelton is also a consultant at Epiphanies Inc., where he effectively uses the action research model to help build and strengthen educational outreach programs.

Breinigsville, PA USA
16 November 2010
249411BV00003B/1/P